D1554392

HOPE

in Our Hearts

HOPE

in Our Hearts

RUSSELL M. NELSON

DESERET
BOOK

SALT LAKE CITY, UTAH

Library of Congress Cataloging-in-Publication Data

Nelson, Russell Marion.
    Hope in our hearts / Russell M. Nelson.
        p. cm.
    Includes bibliographical references and index.
    ISBN 978-1-60641-201-5 (hardbound : alk. paper)
    1. Christian life—Mormon authors.   2. Church of Jesus Christ of
Latter-day Saints—Doctrines.   I. Title.
    BX8656.N46 2009
    248.4'893—dc22   2009027986

Printed in the United States of America
Publishers Printing, Salt Lake City, UT

10   9   8   7   6   5   4   3   2   1

Contents

PERSONAL GROWTH

Introduction

Beginnings, Happenings, and Endurings

Much can be learned from studying the lives and writings of those who strive to follow the Lord Jesus Christ. Knowing men and women of faith fosters faith. Their thoughts, deeds, and teachings can evoke feelings and spark insights that may help another individual be a better disciple.

People of faith may draw strength from the faith of their ancestors. That has surely been true for me. All eight of my great-grandparents were converts to The Church of Jesus Christ of Latter-day Saints in Northern Europe—two from England, two from Denmark, one from Sweden, and three from Norway. Each of them has a story that is precious to me. Also precious to me are my four grandparents, whom I honor and love. The courage they displayed had its roots in testimony, for each discovered the truth that the living Lord has restored His priesthood and guides us today through living prophets and apostles. All these progenitors chose to follow the Lord Jesus Christ with all their heart, mind, and strength.

My beloved parents supported me in my decision to become a medical doctor, and they were enthusiastic about my desire to marry Dantzel White. They encouraged us as we pursued opportunities for advanced education and research that took us from Utah to live in Minneapolis, Minnesota; Washington, D.C.; Boston, Massachusetts; and back to Minneapolis before we returned to Utah, where we made our permanent home. Our parents were excited with the arrival of each of our ten children. Without the unending support of all of our family members, from progenitors to posterity, my life would not have developed the way it did. I am eternally grateful for each of them.

President Spencer W. Kimball, who had entrusted his life to my surgical care, once asked me if I had written the story of my life. I answered, "No."

"You should," he replied. "You will be an ancestor to a large posterity. They must know of your beginnings, your happenings, and your endurings."

With that admonition from this beloved leader, I complied. My autobiography, *From Heart to Heart,* was prepared for the family as a sign of my obedience to the specific request of a prophet of the Lord.[1] It was published in 1979 when I was fifty-four years of age. The book documented my ancestry, childhood, youth, courtship, marriage, military service, education, career, and service to family, community, and church.

During the subsequent quarter of a century, I served as a Regional Representative for five years and as a member of the Quorum of the Twelve Apostles for nearly twenty years. To document that additional history, I invited Elder Spencer J. Condie

Dantzel White and Russell Nelson at the time of their engagement, 1945.

Russell M. Nelson when he was serving as a stake president, 1964.

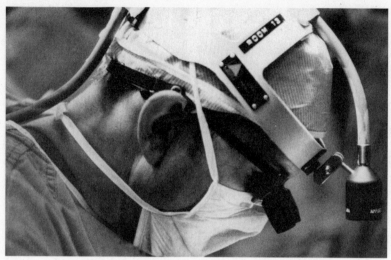

Russell M. Nelson in the operating room, around 1982.
Photo by Dr. Glen Griffin.

of the Seventy to update the story of my life. That biography is titled *Russell M. Nelson: Father, Surgeon, Apostle,* and it was published in 2003.[2] Elder Condie dedicated the book "To Dantzel, Elder Russell M. Nelson's wonderful wife, caring confidante, courageous companion, faithful friend."

Less than two years after that book was published, my dear eternal companion, Dantzel, was suddenly called home to our Heavenly Father. Words cannot describe the stunning and numbing effect of her passing. In a very real way, when she died, part of me died also. The part that remained can never be the same. My grief was mercifully assuaged somewhat by a remarkable outpouring of love from family and friends. They also sensed a deep debt of gratitude for Dantzel and the many blessings that had come to each of us because of her. Expressions of love and consolation came from all parts of the world. Those messages were most comforting.

But my ultimate consolation came from the Lord. Because of

The Nelson family. Standing, left to right: Wendy, Laurie, Marjorie,
Russell Jr., Rosalie. Seated, left to right: Brenda, Emily,
Dantzel, Russell, Gloria, Marsha, Sylvia.

Russell and Dantzel Nelson,
around 1972.

His infinite Atonement, my knowledge was and is ever certain that resurrection is a reality and eternal life a possibility for everyone. That possibility can become a reality as we qualify for eternal life in the presence of our Eternal Father through obedience to the covenants and ordinances of the holy temple. This Dantzel had accomplished. She was thoroughly prepared to return to her Maker.

People react in different ways to the wrenching loss and stark loneliness imposed when an eternal companion is taken to the other side. The commandment to "endure to the end"

(1 Nephi 13:37; 22:31; 2 Nephi 31:16, 20; 33:4; Omni 1:26; 3 Nephi 15:9; Mormon 9:29; D&C 14:7; 18:22; 20:25, 29) is especially difficult to obey when one's loss is unbearably painful. Even among the Apostles, that situation has been endured in different ways. Each faces the future as a widower in his own way, prayerfully and faithfully.

I consulted with my leaders in the Church about how I should move forward. They didn't presume to give me specific direction, declaring that this matter is a personal one. But they did opine that it would be easier to assign me wherever I might be needed if I had a companion by my side. My desire, of course, has always been to serve the Lord. Whether I serve here or on the other side of the veil matters not to me. That decision is the Lord's.

On April 6, 2006, President Gordon B. Hinckley performed the sealing ordinance that brought Sister Wendy Lee Watson and me together at the altar of the holy temple. Privately and sacredly, each of us knew that the Lord was our matchmaker and that our companionship would benefit us, our families, and the Church.

When marriage did not come to Wendy during her young adult years as she supposed and hoped it would, she pursued first her master's and then her doctoral degrees. Her hope was to strengthen families by teaching postgraduate students studying marriage and family therapy. In addition to these academic responsibilities as a university professor, she also had a private practice counseling those whose marriage and family relationships needed healing. Over the years, she helped literally thousands of families.

I was now past eighty with a large family of children, grandchildren, and great-grandchildren, plus eleven beloved brothers in the Quorum of the Twelve Apostles. With so many new

Russell M. and Wendy Watson Nelson, April 2008.
Photo by Danny Boyce Butler.

people to learn to love, no ordinary woman would agree to such an enormous undertaking. But Wendy is extraordinary. She plunged forward in faith, having received her confirmation that the Lord had brought us together.

This I have long known: As a husband and wife immerse themselves deeply and totally in their love of the Lord, their capacity to love each other will increase. Those who put the Lord first will be rewarded eternally for so structuring and self-lessly styling their marriage.

All of God's children encounter challenges and frustrations in life. That is part of our mortal experience. We also know that truly faithful people are produced not by fleeting flashes of exuberant effort but by continuous consistency in keeping the commandments of God. As we follow Jesus Christ, pressing

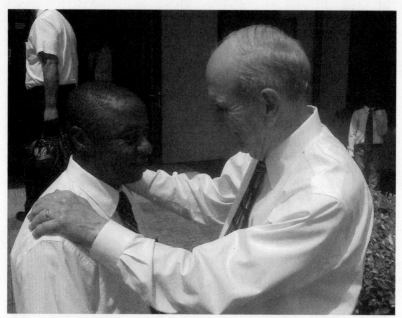

*Russell M. Nelson with Godwin Obi Bassey, the new president
of the Calabar Nigeria Stake, May 2009.*

forward one step at a time, we can do all that the Lord would have us do. Faithfully, He strengthens us!

This is how we are fortified for whatever challenges may come. If one keeps focused on things of eternal significance, the daily ups and downs of life will be properly prioritized. Then we can comprehend that infinite blessings are in store for us in the celestial kingdom.

There will be no second-class recipients of the celestial glory of God. Eternal life is the greatest gift that God can give to His faithful children. Our blessings there will be glorious beyond description. Our only concern now need be that of individual righteousness, preparation, and qualification for those blessings.

So how do we qualify? From time to time we encounter people who wonder about such principles as justification, sanctification, and grace. Important as these are, they are largely in the hands of Almighty God. It would be better for us to focus our efforts on those things over which *we* have control, such as personal faith, repentance, and qualification for temple ordinances and covenants. That done, we can totally trust our loving and merciful Heavenly Father to extend to us what gifts of grace we need in order to return to Him.

Grace is granted to us as we conform to God's standards of personal righteousness. In fact, He commands us to "grow in grace" (D&C 50:40) until we are sanctified and justified "through the grace of our Lord and Savior Jesus Christ" (D&C 20:30–31). In this, as in all things, the Savior set the example. He received grace for grace until finally he gained the fulness of the Father (D&C 93:12–14). And so can we. The Lord declared, "If you keep my commandments you shall receive of his fulness, and be glorified in me as I am in the Father; therefore, I say unto you, you shall receive grace for grace" (D&C 93:20).

One of the great gifts God has given me is a testimony that the Church of Jesus Christ has been restored in this last dispensation and that it is led by living prophets. There have been many previous dispensations. In each of those dispensations, the Lord has chosen to teach His children through prophets. He could have designated some other way, but He chose to reveal His word through ordinary men charged with that extraordinary calling.

In our day, the Lord declared, "This generation shall have my word through" the Prophet Joseph Smith (D&C 5:10). I know Joseph Smith is the Prophet of the Restoration. Through him the gospel of Jesus Christ has been restored to the earth. The Book of Mormon stands as tangible evidence of his prophetic prowess, for he translated it through the gift and power of God. Attestation of that fact came from heaven. Referring to Joseph Smith the Lord declared, "He has translated the book, even that part which I have commanded him, and as your Lord and your God liveth it is true" (D&C 17:6).

While Jesus Christ and His restored gospel are the foundation of my faith, that faith has not been static. In some ways, it is unique. Each Apostle has a different background of beginnings, a widely divergent dossier of happenings and personal challenges to endure. From those beginnings, happenings, and endurings, he forges a faith that allows him to serve as a special witness of the name of the Lord in all the world (D&C 107:23).

Finally, as a lasting legacy to his family, friends, and fellow believers, an Apostle may bequeath his testimony and his teachings. His messages, such as those compiled in this book, are assembled with the hope that others may be edified. My greatest desire is to be a worthy disciple who willingly follows the Lord Jesus Christ. If my testimony and the teachings in this book prompt anyone to follow Him more diligently, I will be most grateful.

Notes

1. Russell M. Nelson, *From Heart to Heart* (Salt Lake City: Quality Press, 1979).

2. Spencer J. Condie, *Russell M. Nelson: Father, Surgeon, Apostle* (Salt Lake City: Deseret Book, 2003).

Relationships
and Family

1

Our Sacred Duty to Honor Women

When I was a young university student, one of my classmates urgently pleaded with a group of us—his Latter-day Saint friends—to donate blood for his mother, who was bleeding profusely. We went directly to the hospital to have our blood typed and tested. I'll never forget our shock when we were told that one of the prospective donors was unfit because of a positive blood test for a sexually transmitted disease. That infected blood belonged to that very classmate whose mother was in trouble! Fortunately, his mother survived, but I'll never forget his lingering sorrow. He bore the burden of knowing that his personal immorality had disqualified him from giving needed aid to his mother, and he had added to her grief. I learned a great lesson: If one dishonors the commandments of God, one dishonors mother; and if one dishonors mother, one dishonors the commandments of God.[1]

Honor Motherhood

During my professional career as a doctor of medicine, I was occasionally asked why I chose to do that difficult work. I responded with my opinion that the highest and noblest work in this life is that of a mother. Since that option was not available to me, I thought that caring for the sick might come close. I tried to care for my patients as compassionately and competently as Mother cared for me.

Many years ago the First Presidency issued a statement that has had a profound and lasting influence upon me. "Motherhood," they wrote, "is near to divinity. It is the highest, holiest service to be assumed by mankind. It places her who honors its holy calling and service next to the angels."[2]

Because mothers are essential to God's great plan of happiness, their sacred work is opposed by Satan, who would destroy the family and demean the worth of women.

You young men need to know that you can hardly achieve your highest potential without the influence of good women, particularly your mother and, in a few years, a good wife. Learn now to show respect and gratitude. Remember that your mother is your *mother.* She should not need to issue orders. Her wish, her hope, her hint should provide direction that you would honor. Thank her and express your love for her. And if she is struggling to rear you without your father, you have a double duty to honor her.

The influence of your mother will bless you throughout life, especially when you serve as a missionary. Long years ago, Elder Frank Croft was serving in the state of Alabama. While preaching to the people, he was forcefully abducted by a vicious gang to be whipped and lashed across his bare back. Elder Croft was ordered to remove his coat and shirt before he was tied to a tree. As he did so, a letter he had recently received from his mother fell to the ground. The vile leader of the gang picked up the letter. Elder Croft closed his eyes and uttered a silent prayer. The attacker read the letter from Elder Croft's mother. From a copy of that letter, I quote:

"My beloved son, . . . remember the words of the Savior when He said, . . . 'Blessed are ye when men shall revile you and persecute you and say all manner of evil against you falsely for my name's sake. Rejoice and be exceedingly glad for you will have your reward in Heaven for so persecuted they the prophets which were before you.' Also remember the Savior upon the cross suffering from the sins of the world when He had uttered these immortal words, 'Father forgive them, for they know not what they do.' Surely, my boy, they who are mistreating you . . . know not what they do or they would not do it. Sometime, somewhere, they will understand and then they will regret their action and they will honor you for the glorious work you are doing. So be patient, my son, love those who mistreat you and say all manner of evil against you and the Lord will bless you and magnify you. . . . Remember also, my son, that day and night, your mother is praying for you."

Elder Croft watched the hateful man as he studied the letter. He would read a line or two, then sit and ponder. He arose to approach his captive. The man said:

"Feller, you must have a wonderful mother. You see, I once had one, too."

Then, addressing the mob, he said: "Men, after reading this Mormon's mother's letter, I just can't go ahead with the job. Maybe we had better let him go." Elder Croft was released without harm.[3]

We are deeply grateful for the faithful mothers and fathers

of our wonderful missionaries. The love they bear for their children is sublime.

Honor the Sisters

We who bear the holy priesthood have a sacred duty to honor our sisters. We are old enough and wise enough to know that teasing is wrong. We respect sisters—not only in our immediate families but also all the wonderful sisters in our lives. As daughters of God, their potential is divine. Without them, eternal life would be impossible. Our high regard for them should spring from our love of God and from an awareness of their lofty purpose in His great eternal plan.

Hence, I warn against pornography. It is degrading of women. It is evil. It is infectious, destructive, and addictive. The body has means by which it can cleanse itself from harmful effects of contaminated food or drink. But it cannot vomit back the poison of pornography. Once recorded, it always remains subject to recall, flashing its perverted images across your mind, with power to draw you away from the wholesome things in life. Avoid it like the plague!

Honor Your Wife

To you who are not yet married, think about your future marriage. Choose your companion well. Remember the scriptures that teach the importance of marriage in the temple:

"In the celestial glory there are three heavens or degrees; and in order to obtain the highest, a man must enter into this order of the priesthood [meaning the new and everlasting covenant of marriage]; and if he does not, he cannot obtain it" (D&C 131:1–3).

The highest ordinances in the house of the Lord are received by husband and wife together and equally—or not at all!

In retrospect I see that the most important day of my life was the day when my sweetheart, Dantzel, and I were married in the holy temple. Without her I could not have the highest and most enduring blessings of the priesthood. Without her I would not be the father to our wonderful children or the grandfather to our precious grandchildren.

As fathers we should have love unbounded for the mothers of our children. We should accord to them the gratitude, respect, and praise that they deserve.

Husbands, to keep alive the spirit of romance in your marriage, be considerate and kind in the tender intimacies of your married life. Let your thoughts and actions inspire confidence and trust. Let your words be wholesome and your time together be uplifting. Let nothing in life take priority over your wife— not work, recreation, or hobby.

An ideal marriage is a true partnership between two imperfect people, each striving to complement the other, to keep the commandments, and to do the will of the Lord.

Fathers Preside Over the Family in Love

The family is the most important unit of society and of the Church. The family is ordained of God. It is central to His plan "for the eternal destiny of His children."[4] "God has established families to bring happiness to His children, allow them to learn correct principles in a loving atmosphere, and prepare them for eternal life."[5]

Parents have the primary responsibility for the welfare of their children (D&C 68:25–28). The Church does not replace that parental responsibility. Ideally, the Latter-day Saint family is presided over by a worthy man who holds the priesthood. This patriarchal authority has been honored among the people of God in all dispensations. It is of divine origin, and the union of a family, if sealed by proper authority, will continue throughout eternity. He who is the Father of us all and the source of this authority demands that governance in the home be in love and righteousness (D&C 121:41–45).

You fathers can help with the dishes, care for a crying baby, and change a diaper. And perhaps some Sunday you could get the children ready for Church, and your wife could sit in the car and honk.

"Husbands, love your wives, even as Christ also loved the church, and gave himself for it" (Ephesians 5:25). With that kind of love, we will be better husbands and fathers, more loving and spiritual leaders. Happiness at home is most likely to be achieved when practices there are founded upon the teachings of Jesus Christ.[6] Ours is the responsibility to ensure that we have family prayer, family scripture study, and family home evening. Ours is the responsibility to prepare our children to receive the ordinances of salvation and exaltation and the blessings promised to tithe payers. Ours is the privilege to bestow priesthood blessings of healing, comfort, and direction.

The home is the great laboratory of love. There the raw chemicals of selfishness and greed are melded in the crucible of cooperation to yield compassionate concern and love one for another (Mosiah 4:14–15; D&C 68:25–31).

Honor the special sisters in your lives. Express your love to your wife, to your mother, and to the sisters. Praise them for their forbearance with you even when you are not at your best.

Thank the Lord for these sisters who—like our Heavenly Father—love us not only for what we are but also for what we may become. Humbly I thank God for my mother, my sisters, my daughters, my granddaughters, and my special sweetheart, companion, and friend—my wife!

May God bless us to honor each virtuous woman.

NOTES

From a talk given at general conference, April 1999.

1. Many scriptures teach us to honor our parents, including Exodus 20:12; Deuteronomy 5:16; Matthew 15:4; 19:19; Mark 7:10; 10:19; Luke 18:20; Ephesians 6:2; 1 Nephi 17:55; Mosiah 13:20; JST, Matthew 19:19; JST, Mark 7:12, Bible appendix.
2. In James R. Clark, comp., *Messages of the First Presidency of The Church of Jesus Christ of Latter-day Saints,* 6 vols. (1965–75), 6:178. In 1935 the First Presidency stated, "The true spirit of The Church of Jesus Christ of Latter-day Saints gives to woman the highest place of honor in human life" (in *Messages of the First Presidency,* 6:5).
3. See Arthur M. Richardson, *The Life and Ministry of John Morgan* (n.p., 1965), 267–68.
4. "The Family: A Proclamation to the World," *Ensign,* November 1995, 102, paragraph one.
5. *Family Guidebook* (Salt Lake City: The Church of Jesus Christ of Latter-day Saints, 1992), 1.
6. See "The Family: A Proclamation to the World," 102, paragraph seven.

2

Set in Order Thy House

Years ago when Sister Nelson and I had several teenage daughters, we took our family on a vacation far away from telephones and boyfriends. We went on a raft trip down the Colorado River through the Grand Canyon. As we started our journey, we had no idea how dangerous this trip could be.

The first day was beautiful. But on the second day, when we approached Horn Creek Rapids and saw a precipitous drop ahead, I was terrified. Floating on a rubber raft, our precious family was about to plunge over a waterfall! Instinctively I put one arm around my wife and the other around our youngest daughter. To protect them, I tried to hold them close to me. But as we reached the precipice, the bended raft became a giant sling and shot me into the air. I landed into the roiling rapids of the river. I had a hard time coming up. Each time I tried to find air, I hit the underside of the raft. My family couldn't see me, but I could hear them shouting, "Daddy! Where's Daddy?"

I finally found the side of the raft and rose to the surface. The family pulled my nearly drowned body out of the water. We were thankful to be safely reunited.

The next several days were pleasant and delightful. Then came the last day, when we were to go over Lava Falls, known as the most dangerous drop of the journey. When I saw what was ahead, I immediately asked to beach the raft and hold an emergency family council, knowing that if we were to survive this experience, we needed to plan carefully. I reasoned with our family: "No matter what happens, the rubber raft will remain on top of the water. If we cling with all our might to ropes secured to the raft, we can make it. Even if the raft should capsize, we will be all right if we hang tightly to the ropes."

I turned to our little seven-year-old daughter and said, "All of the others will cling to a rope. But you will need to hold on to your daddy. Sit behind me. Put your arms around me, and hold me tightly while I hold the rope."

That we did. We crossed those steep, rough rapids— hanging on for dear life—and all of us made it safely.[1]

The Lesson

Brothers and sisters, I nearly lost my life learning a lesson that I now give to you. As we go through life, even through very rough waters, a father's instinctive impulse to cling tightly to his wife and to his children may not be the best way to accomplish his objective. Instead, if he will lovingly cling to the Savior and the iron rod of the gospel, his family will want to cling to him and to the Savior.

This lesson is surely not limited to fathers. Regardless of gender, marital status, or age, individuals can choose to link themselves directly to the Savior, hold fast to the rod of His truth, and lead by the light of that truth. By so doing, they become examples of righteousness to whom others will want to cling.

The Commandment

With the Lord, families are essential. He created the earth that we could gain physical bodies and form families (D&C 2:1–3). He established His Church to exalt families. He provides temples so that families can be together forever (D&C 138:47–48).

Of course, He expects fathers to preside over, provide for, and protect their families (1 Timothy 5:8). But the Master has asked for much more. Etched in sacred scripture is a commandment to "set in order thy house" (D&C 93:44; see also 2 Kings 20:1; 2 Chronicles 32:32; Isaiah 38:1). Once we as parents understand the importance and meaning of that commandment, we need to learn how to do it.

How to Set Your House in Order

To set our house in an order pleasing to the Lord, we need to do it His way. We are to employ His attributes of "righteousness, godliness, faith, love, patience, [and] meekness" (1 Timothy 6:11). Each father should remember that "no power or influence can or ought to be maintained by virtue of the priesthood, only by persuasion, by long-suffering, by gentleness and meekness, and by love unfeigned" (D&C 121:41).

Parents are to be living examples of "kindness, and pure

knowledge, which . . . greatly enlarge the soul" (D&C 121:42). Each mother and father should lay aside selfish interests and avoid any thought of hypocrisy, physical force, or evil speaking (1 Peter 2:1). Parents soon learn that each child has an inborn yearning to be free. Each individual wants to make his or her own way. No one wants to be restrained, even by a well-intentioned parent. But all of us can cling to the Lord.

Ages ago, Job taught that concept. He said, "My righteousness I hold fast, and will not let it go" (Job 27:6). Nephi also taught, "Whoso would hearken unto the word of God, and . . . hold fast unto it . . . would never perish" (1 Nephi 15:24).

These tenets are timeless as the gospel and endless as eternity. Ponder these additional scriptural admonitions:

From the Old Testament Proverbs we read, "Take fast hold of instruction; let her not go: keep her; for she is thy life" (Proverbs 4:13). From the New Testament we read: "Brethren, stand fast, and hold the traditions which ye have been taught" (2 Thessalonians 2:15). Other related scriptures include "Hold fast the . . . sound words, which thou hast heard of me, in faith and love which is in Christ Jesus" (2 Timothy 1:13) and "Let us hold fast the profession of our faith without wavering" (Hebrews 10:23).

From the Book of Mormon we learn about multitudes that were "continually holding fast to the rod of iron" (1 Nephi 8:30), likening it to "the word of God" (1 Nephi 11:25). Anchored in truth, that iron rod is immovable and immutable.

Other Divine Mandates

Not only are parents to cling to the word of the Lord, but they also have a divine mandate to teach it to their children.

Scriptural direction is clear: "Inasmuch as parents have children in Zion . . . that teach them *not* to understand the doctrine of repentance, faith in Christ the Son of the living God, and of baptism and the gift of the Holy Ghost by the laying on of the hands, when eight years old, the sin be upon the heads of the parents" (D&C 68:25; emphasis added).

That commandment places responsibility and accountability for the teaching of children squarely upon the shoulders of the parents. The proclamation to the world regarding the family warns that individuals "who fail to fulfill family responsibilities will one day stand accountable before God."[2] I solemnly reaffirm that reality.

In discharging these duties, we need both the Church and the family. They work hand in hand to strengthen each other. The Church exists to exalt the family, and the family is the fundamental unit of the Church.

These interrelationships are evident as we study the early history of the Church. In 1833 the Lord rebuked young leaders of His Church because of parental shortcomings. He said:

"I have commanded you to bring up your children in light and truth. But verily I say unto you, . . . you have not taught your children light and truth, according to the commandments. . . . And now a commandment I give unto you . . . you shall set in order your own house, for there are many things that are not right in your house. . . . First set in order thy house" (D&C 93:40–44).

This revelation represents one of the many powerful validations of the integrity of the Prophet Joseph Smith. He did not delete from scripture words of stinging rebuke, even though some were directed to him (D&C 93:47).

In our day the First Presidency has again stressed parental priority. In a recent letter to the Saints, they state: "We call upon parents to devote their best efforts to the teaching and rearing of their children in gospel principles which will keep them close to the Church. The home is the basis of a righteous life, and no other instrumentality can take its place or fulfill its essential functions in carrying forward this God-given responsibility."[3]

What Should Parents Teach?

With this sacred charge in mind, let us consider what we should teach. Scriptures direct parents to teach faith in Jesus Christ, repentance, baptism, and the gift of the Holy Ghost (Moroni 8:10; D&C 19:31; 68:25–34; 138:33; Articles of Faith 1:4). Parents are to teach the plan of salvation (Moses 6:58–62) and the importance of living in complete accord with the commandments of God (Leviticus 10:11; Deuteronomy 6:7; Mosiah 4:14). Otherwise, their children will surely suffer in ignorance of God's redeeming and liberating law (2 Nephi 2:26; Mosiah 1:3; 5:8; D&C 98:8). Parents should also teach by example how to consecrate their lives—using their time, talents, tithing, and substance (Mosiah 4:21–26; 18:27; Alma 1:27) to establish the Church and kingdom of God upon the earth (JST, Matthew 6:38). Parents who live in that manner will literally bless their posterity. A scripture states, "Thy duty is unto the church forever, and this because of thy family" (D&C 23:3).

Opposition to the Family

Parents and children should realize that strong opposition will always come against the work and will of the Lord (Moroni

7:12–19). Because the work—and glory—of God is to bring to pass our immortality and eternal life as a family (Moses 1:39), it logically follows that the work of the adversary will strike directly at the heart of the home—the family. Relentlessly Lucifer attacks the sanctity of life and the joy of parenthood.

Because the evil one is ever at work, our vigilance cannot be relaxed—not even for a moment. A small and seemingly innocent invitation can turn into a tall temptation that can lead to tragic transgression. Night and day, at home or away, we must shun sin and "hold fast that which is good" (1 Thessalonians 5:21).

The seditious evils of pornography, abortion, and addiction to harmful substances serve as termites to erode the undergirding strength of a happy home and a faithful family. We cannot yield to any iniquity without putting our families at risk.

Satan wants us to be miserable just as he is (2 Nephi 2:17–18, 27). He would animate our carnal appetites, entice us to live in spiritual darkness, and encourage us to doubt the reality of life after death. The Apostle Paul observed, "If in this life only we have hope in Christ, we are of all men most miserable" (1 Corinthians 15:19).

Perpetuation of Family Blessings

An understanding of God's great plan of happiness, however, fortifies our faith in the future. His plan provides answers to ageless questions: Are all our sympathies and love for each other only temporary—to be lost in death? No! Can family life endure beyond this period of mortal probation? Yes! God has revealed the eternal nature of celestial marriage and the family as the source of our greatest joy.

Material possessions and honors of the world do not endure. But our union as wife, husband, and family can. The only duration of family life that satisfies the loftiest longings of the human soul is forever. No sacrifice is too great to have the blessings of an eternal marriage. To qualify, one needs only to deny oneself of ungodliness and honor the ordinances of the temple. By making and keeping sacred temple covenants, we evidence our love for God, for our companion, and for our posterity— even those yet unborn. Our family is the focus of our greatest work and joy in this life; so will it be throughout all eternity, when we can "inherit thrones, kingdoms, principalities, . . . powers, dominions, . . . exaltation and glory" (D&C 132:19).

These priceless blessings can be ours if we set our houses in order now and faithfully cling to the gospel. God lives. Jesus is the Christ. This is His Church.

Notes

From a talk given at general conference, October 2001.

1. See Russell M. Nelson and Rebecca M. Taylor, "Friend to Friend," *Friend,* March 1997, 6–7.
2. "The Family: A Proclamation to the World," *Ensign,* November 1995, 102, paragraph 9.
3. In that letter, dated February 11, 1999, and signed by Presidents Gordon B. Hinckley, Thomas S. Monson, and James E. Faust, they also described what parents might do: "We counsel parents and children to give highest priority to family prayer, family home evening, gospel study and instruction, and wholesome family activities. However worthy and appropriate other demands or activities may be, they must not be permitted to displace the divinely appointed duties that only parents and families can adequately perform" (in "Policies, Announcements, and Appointments," *Ensign,* June 1999, 80).

3

Roots and Branches

Each time we experience security checks at an airport, we are asked to show photographic identification. We understand the need and comply, knowing that it is necessary and helpful. But I submit my photograph as evidence of my true identity somewhat apologetically. If someone were to examine my passport photo and say that it's a good likeness, I would know it's time to go home. But I feel apologetic for another reason. The photo shows nothing about my roots and branches. They are important parts of my identity.

Could you tell much about a tree by looking at a photograph of only its trunk? No! Roots and branches of trees provide much more information. So it is with us both *personally* and with *our religion*.

Personal Roots

Personal roots are really important. Sister Nelson and I know a family that proudly displays evidence of their ancestral roots with large paintings portrayed on the *outside* walls of their home. Beautiful artwork there depicts distinctive patterns of identity for both of their family lines.

When relatives gather around a new baby, one inevitably hears comments such as "She has red hair, just like her mother," or "He has a dimple in his chin, just like his father."

Each of us has ancestral roots. Each man has received some genetic markers that are just like those of his father. Each woman has received some genetic markers that are just like those of her mother.[1] In addition, each of us has received other genetic gifts that make us unique.

Because we have a spirit as well as a physical body (D&C 88:15), we also have spiritual roots that go way back. They shape our values, our beliefs, and our faith. Spiritual roots guide our commitment to the ideals and teachings of the Lord (Ephesians 3:14–19; Colossians 2:6–7).

Most children have a natural desire to emulate the examples of their parents. Generally, boys incline toward the attitudes and work of their fathers; girls aspire to live as their mothers do. Parents, don't be too surprised if, sometime along the way, your children become better than you.

Personal roots, physical and spiritual, merit gratitude. For my life, I am grateful to my Creator as well as to my dear parents and progenitors. I try to honor them by learning of them and serving them in the temple (D&C 128:15). Parents have a responsibility to share knowledge of their personal roots with their children and grandchildren. Learning their history together unifies a family.

Religious Roots

We also need to know the roots of our religion. The Church of Jesus Christ of Latter-day Saints, though officially organized in 1830, was restored from roots that also go way back. Truths from previous dispensations have now been gathered, amplified, and clarified (D&C 128:18). For us as parents and teachers, we have an excellent teaching resource in the Articles of Faith. Written by the Prophet Joseph Smith,[2] this document refers to many doctrines that undergird our religion. It mentions the Godhead, moral agency, the Fall of Adam, and the Atonement of Jesus Christ. It spells out the foundational principles and ordinances of faith, repentance, baptism, and the laying on of hands for the gift of the Holy Ghost. It addresses matters of priesthood authority and organization. It notes as sacred scripture the Holy Bible, the Book of Mormon, and an open canon of continuing revelation from God. And it proclaims the actuality of the gathering of Israel.[3] What a treasure-house of truth is this precious document for teaching our religious roots.

Other revealed doctrines at the root of our religion offer light on the Creation, the Resurrection, the law of tithing, prayer, and the consummate blessings of the temple. As we teach these doctrines, we realize how firm is our foundation. As we apply these doctrines in our lives, the roots of our religion become part of our own spiritual strength.

Converts to the Church also need to strengthen their religious roots. President Gordon B. Hinckley taught that each convert needs a friend, a responsibility, and nurturing by the good word of God. With such roots to support them and their children, precious converts become pioneers for their own families to follow.

Unfortunately, some members of faithful families drift away because their own roots are weak. My heart aches when I learn of those who turn from the faith of their pioneer predecessors. One professionally acclaimed friend and gifted son of faithful ancestors has allowed one doctrinal doubt to dim his view of the fulness of the gospel and drive an ever-widening wedge between him and the temple. Another acquaintance, a sweet sister with illustrious pioneer progenitors, now politely states that she is not a "practicing member" of the Church.

Have these dear people become so fashionable that they have forgotten their roots? Have they forgotten what the Restoration really means and what it cost? Have they forgotten their pioneer heritage and their lineage as declared in patriarchal blessings? For a few fleeting favors now, would they forget and forfeit eternal life? Forgetful of the roots that have blessed them, they no longer enjoy the spiritual sparkle of Saints engaged in the work of Almighty God.

Their noble ancestors "were brought to the knowledge of the truth, . . . according to the spirit of revelation and of prophecy, and the power of God." Their forebears "were converted unto the Lord [and] never did fall away" (Alma 23:6). How will those progenitors feel about the drift of their descendants? Their disappointment will likely turn to sorrow, for fruit detached from roots cannot long survive.

The Lord issued this solemn warning:

"After ye have been nourished by the good word of God . . . , will ye reject these words . . . of the prophets; and will ye reject all the words which have been spoken concerning Christ, . . . the power of God, and the gift of the Holy Ghost, . . . and make a mock of the great plan of redemption, which [has] been laid for you?

" . . . The resurrection . . . will bring you to stand with shame and awful guilt before the bar of God" (Jacob 6:7–9).

I plead with each of us to heed that sacred warning.

Personal Branches

Just as our roots determine to a significant degree who we are, our branches are also an important extension of our identity. Personal branches bear the fruit of our loins (2 Nephi 3:6–7). Scriptures teach, "By their fruits ye shall know them" (Matthew 7:20; 3 Nephi 14:20; see also JST, Matthew 7:25). Earlier in life Sister Nelson and I often met young people who said they felt as if they knew us because they knew our children. Now we are greeted fondly by those who know us because they know our grandchildren.

Religious Branches

In much the same way, our religion is known by the fruit of its branches. Recently I met with government officials from a land far from here who were deeply impressed with the Church and its efforts throughout the world. They liked our teachings about the family and wanted copies of our proclamation on the family and guidebooks for family home evening. They wanted to know more about our welfare program and humanitarian help. We complied as we could and then shifted attention from *what* we do to *why* we do it. I explained with an analogy to a tree. "You are attracted by various fruits of our faith," I said. "They are plentiful and powerful. But you cannot savor this fruit unless you know the tree that produces it. And you cannot understand the tree unless you comprehend its roots. With our religion, you cannot have the fruits without the roots." This they understood.

Fruits from the branching tree of the gospel include "love, joy, peace, longsuffering, gentleness, goodness, [and] faith" (Galatians 5:22). President Harold B. Lee once said: "Beautiful, luscious fruit does not grow unless the roots of the . . . tree have been planted in rich, fertile soil and unless due care is given to proper pruning, cultivation, and irrigation. So likewise the luscious fruits of virtue and chastity, honesty, temperance, integrity, and fidelity are not to be found growing in that individual whose life is not founded on a firm testimony of the truths of the gospel and of the life and the mission of the Lord Jesus Christ."[4]

The fruits of the gospel are delicious to those who obey the Lord. We pursue an education knowing that "the glory of God is intelligence" (D&C 93:36). The blessing of tithing comes by paying tithing (Malachi 3:10; 3 Nephi 24:10). Rewards are reaped from the Word of Wisdom by obedience to it (D&C 89:18–21). We learn from experience borne of gospel living that prayer, honoring the Sabbath day, and partaking of the sacrament protect us from the bondage of sin. We shun pornography and immorality, knowing that the peace of personal purity can be ours only as we live according to the laws of the gospel.

The Lord gave this promise and commandment: "Now ye are clean through the word which I have spoken unto you. . . . Abide in me, and I in you. . . . I am the vine, ye are the branches" (John 15:3–5). Simply summarized, life's greatest blessings will come to us if our love of Jesus Christ is rooted deeply in our hearts (Ephesians 3:17).

Testimony

Personal identity is much more than a passport photograph. Divinity is rooted in each of us. "We all are the work of [our Creator's] hand" (Isaiah 64:8). We are eternal beings. In premortal realms, men were foreordained to priesthood responsibilities (Alma 13:1–5). Before the foundation of the world, women were prepared that they might bear children and glorify God (D&C 132:63).

We came to this mortal experience to acquire a body and to be tried and tested.[5] We are to form families and be sealed in holy temples, with joy and loving relationships that endure eternally. To these everlasting truths, we are personally rooted.

Branches of our families and of the gospel bear fruit to enrich our lives. God's work and His glory—"to bring to pass the immortality and eternal life of man" (Moses 1:39)—can become ours. We can dwell with Him and with our families forever. Those blessings will be granted to the faithful in His own way and time (D&C 88:68).[6]

God lives. Jesus is the Christ. Joseph Smith is the revelator and prophet of this last dispensation. The Book of Mormon is true. The Church of Jesus Christ of Latter-day Saints is the Lord's kingdom established once again upon the earth. If rooted to these truths, the fruit of our branches will remain (John 15:16).

NOTES

From a talk given at general conference, April 2004.

1. In addition to the genetic information each child receives from his or her mother and father, a small set of mitochondrial DNA comes from the mother to both her sons and daughters.

2. The Articles of Faith were included in a letter to Mr. John Wentworth, editor and proprietor of a Chicago newspaper, and were first published in the *Times and Seasons,* March 1, 1842; see Joseph Smith Jr., "Gospel Classics: The Wentworth Letter," *Ensign,* July 2002, 26–32.

3. This document also mentions gifts of the Spirit that enlighten lives of members of the Church. It foretells of great events of the latter days, such as the restoration of the ten tribes, the establishment of Zion, and the millennial reign of Jesus Christ upon a renewed earth. It includes principles of freedom of worship, tolerance, and obedience to law, and it concludes with an expression pertaining to our perception of life and of lofty personal ideals.

4. Harold B. Lee, *Stand Ye in Holy Places* (Salt Lake City: Deseret Book, 1974), 218–19.

5. "Even as Abraham" (D&C 101:4; see also Hebrews 11:17).

6. When any blessing is obtained from God, "it is by obedience to that law upon which it is predicated" (D&C 130:21).

4

Nurturing Marriage

As we Brethren travel about the world, sometimes we see worrisome scenes. On a recent flight, I sat behind a husband and wife. She obviously loved her husband. As she stroked the back of his neck I could see her wedding ring. She would nestle close to him and rest her head upon his shoulder, seeking his companionship.

In contrast, he seemed totally oblivious to her presence. He was focused solely upon an electronic game player. During the entire flight, his attention was riveted upon that device. Not once did he look at her, speak to her, or acknowledge her yearning for affection.

His inattention made me feel like shouting: "Open your eyes, man! Can't you see? Pay attention! Your wife loves you! She needs you!"

I don't know more about them. I haven't seen them since.

Perhaps I was alarmed unduly. And possibly, if this man knew of my concern for them, he might feel sorry for me for not knowing how to use his exciting electronic toy.

But these things I do know: I know "that marriage between a man and a woman is ordained of God and that the family is central to the Creator's plan for the eternal destiny of His children."[1] I know that the earth was created and that the Lord's Church was restored so that families could be sealed and exalted as eternal entities.[2] And I know that one of Satan's cunning methods of undermining the work of the Lord is to attack the sacred institutions of marriage and the family.

Marriage brings greater possibilities for happiness than does any other human relationship. Yet some married couples fall short of their full potential. They let their romance become rusty, take each other for granted, and allow other interests or clouds of neglect to obscure their vision of what their marriage really could be. Marriages would be happier if nurtured more carefully.

I realize that many mature members of the Church are not married. Through no failing of their own, they deal with the trials of life alone. May we all remember that in the Lord's own way and time, no blessings will be withheld from His faithful Saints (D&C 49:15–17). For those who are now or will be married, I suggest two steps you can take to have a more joyful marriage.

Doctrinal Foundation

The first step is to comprehend the doctrinal foundation for marriage. The Lord declared that marriage is the legal wedding of one man and one woman:

"Marriage is ordained of God unto man. Wherefore, it is lawful that he should have one wife, and they twain shall be one flesh, and all this that the earth might answer the end of its creation" (D&C 49:15–16).

Worldly trends to define marriage in some other way would sadly serve to destroy the institution of marriage. Such schemes are contrary to the plan of God.

It was He who said, "For this cause shall a man leave father and mother, and shall cleave to his wife: and they twain shall be one flesh" (Matthew 19:5; see also Mark 10:7–8).

Scripture further reaffirms that "the man [is not] without the woman, neither the woman without the man, in the Lord" (1 Corinthians 11:11).

Marriage is the foundry for social order, the fountain of virtue, and the foundation for eternal exaltation. Marriage has been divinely designated as an eternal and everlasting covenant (D&C 132:19). Marriage is sanctified when it is cherished and honored in holiness. That union is not merely between husband and wife; it embraces a partnership with God (Matthew 19:6). "Husband and wife have a solemn responsibility to love and care for each other."[3] Children born of that marital union are "an heritage of the Lord" (Psalm 127:3). Marriage is but the beginning bud of family life; parenthood is its flower. And that flower becomes a beautiful bouquet when graced with grandchildren. Families may become as eternal as the kingdom of God itself (D&C 132:19–20).

Marriage is both a commandment and an exalting principle of the gospel.[4] Because marriage is ordained of God, the intimate physical expressions of married love are sacred. Yet all too commonly, these divine gifts are desecrated. If a couple allows lewd language or pornography to corrupt their intimacy, they offend their Creator while they degrade and diminish their own divine gifts. True happiness is predicated upon personal purity (Alma 41:10). Scripture commands, "Be ye clean" (D&C 38:42; see also Isaiah 52:11; 3 Nephi 20:41; D&C 133:5). Marriage should ever be a covenant to lift husbands and wives to exaltation in celestial glory.

Marriage was intended by the Lord to endure beyond physical death. His plan offers eternal perpetuation of the family in the kingdom of God. His plan provides temples and opportunities to officiate therein for the living and the dead. A marriage sealed there launches a husband and wife into that grand order of unity so necessary to the perfection of God's work (D&C 128:15–18).

Doctrines related to marriage include individual agency and accountability. All of us are accountable for our choices. Couples blessed with children are accountable to God for the care they give to their children.

As I meet with priesthood leaders, I often ask about the priorities of their various responsibilities. Usually they mention the important Church duties to which they have been called. Too few mention their responsibilities at home.

Yet priesthood offices, keys, callings, and quorums are meant to exalt families (D&C 23:3). Priesthood authority has been restored so that families can be sealed eternally. So, brethren, your foremost priesthood duty is to nurture your marriage—to care for, respect, honor, and love your wife. Be a blessing to her and your children.

Strengthening Marriage

With these doctrinal underpinnings in mind, let us consider the second step—specific actions that strengthen a marriage. I will offer suggestions and invite each couple privately to ponder them and adapt them as needed to their particular circumstances.

My suggestions use three action verbs: to *appreciate,* to *communicate,* and to *contemplate.*

To *appreciate*—to say "I love you" and "thank you"—is not difficult. But these expressions of love and appreciation do more than acknowledge a kind thought or deed. They are signs of sweet civility. As grateful partners look for the good in each other and sincerely pay compliments to one another, wives and husbands will strive to become the persons described in those compliments.

Suggestion number two—to *communicate* well with your spouse—is also important. Good communication includes taking time to plan together. Couples need private time to observe, to talk, and to really listen to each other. They need to cooperate—helping each other as equal partners. They need to nurture their spiritual as well as their physical intimacy. They should strive to elevate and motivate each other. Marital unity is sustained when goals are mutually understood. Good communication is also enhanced by prayer. To pray with specific mention of a spouse's good deed (or need) nurtures a marriage.

My third suggestion—to *contemplate*—has deep meaning. It comes from Latin roots *con,* meaning "with," and *templum,* meaning "a space or place to meditate." It is the root from which the word *temple* comes. If couples contemplate often—with each other in the temple—sacred covenants will be better remembered and kept. Frequent participation in temple service and regular family scripture study nourish a marriage and strengthen faith within a family. Contemplation allows us to anticipate and to resonate (or be in tune) with each other and with the Lord. Contemplation will nurture both a marriage and God's kingdom. The Master said, "Seek not the things of this world but seek ye first to build up the kingdom of God, and to establish his righteousness, and all these things shall be added unto you" (JST, Matthew 6:38; see also Matthew 6:33 note a).

I invite each marital partner to consider these suggestions and then determine specific goals to nurture your relationship. Begin with sincere desire. Identify those actions needed to bless your spiritual unity and purpose. Above all, do not be selfish! Generate a spirit of selflessness and generosity. Celebrate and commemorate each day together as a treasured gift from heaven.

President Harold B. Lee said, "The most important of the Lord's work you and I will ever do will be within the walls of our own homes."[5] And President David O. McKay declared, "No other success can compensate for failure in the home."[6]

When you as husband and wife recognize the divine design in your union—when you feel deeply that God has brought you to each other—your vision will be expanded and your understanding enhanced. Such feelings are expressed in words of a song that has long been a favorite of mine:

> *Because you come to me with naught save love,*
> *And hold my hand and lift mine eyes above,*
> *A wider world of hope and joy I see,*
> *Because you come to me.*
> *Because you speak to me in accents sweet,*
> *I find the roses waking round my feet,*
> *And I am led through tears and joy to thee,*
> *Because you speak to me.*
> *Because God made thee mine, I'll cherish thee,*
> *Through light and darkness, through all time to be,*
> *And pray His love may make our love divine,*
> *Because God made thee mine.*[7]

I pray that each marriage may be so nurtured.

NOTES

From a talk given at general conference, April 2006.

1. "The Family: A Proclamation to the World," *Ensign,* November 1995, 102, paragraph one.
2. Whenever scriptures warn that the "earth would be utterly wasted," the warning is connected to the need for priesthood authority to seal families together in holy temples (D&C 2:3; 138:48; Joseph Smith—History 1:39).
3. "The Family: A Proclamation to the World," 102, paragraph 6.
4. See Joseph Fielding Smith, *The Way to Perfection,* 10th ed. (Salt Lake City: Genealogical Society of The Church of Jesus Christ of Latter-day Saints, 1953), 232–33.
5. Harold B. Lee, *Stand Ye in Holy Places* (Salt Lake City: Deseret Book, 1974), 255.
6. In Conference Report, April 1935, 116; quoted from J. E. McCulloch, *Home: The Savior of Civilization* (Washington, D.C.: Southern Co-operative League, 1924), 42.
7. "Because," words by Edward Teschemacher (1902).

5

Celestial Marriage

I n this world abounding with misery, we are truly thankful for God's "great plan of happiness" (Alma 42:8). It is also known as the "plan of . . . God" (2 Nephi 9:13; Alma 34:9), the "plan of redemption" (Jacob 6:8; Alma 12:26, 30, 32–33; 29:2; 42:13), the "plan of salvation" (Alma 24:14; 42:5), and the "plan of mercy" (Alma 42:15, 31). God's plan declares that men and women are "that they might have joy" (2 Nephi 2:25). That joy comes when we choose to live in harmony with His eternal plan.

The importance of choice may be illustrated by a home-spun concept that came to mind one day when I was shopping in a large retail store. I call it "patterns of the shopper." Because shopping is part of our daily life, these patterns may be familiar.

Wise shoppers study their options thoroughly before they make a selection. They focus primarily on the quality and durability of a desired product. They want the very best. In contrast, some shoppers look for bargains, and others may splurge, only to learn later—much to their dismay—that their choice did not endure well. And sadly, there are those rare individuals who cast aside their personal integrity and steal what they want. We call them shoplifters.

The patterns of the shopper may be applied to the topic of marriage. A couple in love can choose a marriage of the highest quality or a lesser type that will not endure. Or they can choose neither and brazenly steal what they want as "marital shoplifters."

The subject of marriage is debated across the world, where various arrangements exist for conjugal living. My purpose in speaking out on this topic is to declare, as an Apostle of the Lord (D&C 107:35), that marriage between a man and a woman is sacred—it is ordained of God (D&C 49:15–17). I also assert the virtue of a temple marriage. It is the highest and most enduring type of marriage that our Creator can offer to His children.

While salvation is an individual matter, exaltation is a family matter.[1] Only those who are married in the temple and whose marriage is sealed by the Holy Spirit of Promise will continue as spouses after death and receive the highest degree of celestial glory, or exaltation (D&C 76:53; 132:7). A temple marriage is also called a celestial marriage. Within the celestial glory are three levels. To obtain the highest, a husband and wife must be sealed for time and all eternity and keep their covenants made in a holy temple (D&C 131:1–3).

The noblest yearning of the human heart is for a marriage that can endure beyond death. Fidelity to a temple marriage does that. It allows families to be together forever.

This goal is glorious. All church activities, advancements, quorums, and classes are means to the end of an exalted family.[2]

To make this goal possible, our Heavenly Father has restored priesthood keys in this dispensation so that essential ordinances in His plan can be performed by proper authority. Heavenly messengers—including John the Baptist (D&C 13); Peter, James, and John (Matthew 16:18–19; D&C 27:12–13; Joseph Smith—History 1:72); Moses, Elias, and Elijah (D&C 110:11–16)—have participated in that restoration (D&C 128:8, 18; 132:45–46).

Knowledge of this revealed truth is spreading across the earth (2 Nephi 10:2; 30:8). We, as the Lord's prophets and apostles, again proclaim to the world that "the family is central to the Creator's plan for the eternal destiny of His children."[3]

We further proclaim that "all human beings—male and female—are created in the image of God. Each is a beloved spirit son or daughter of heavenly parents, and, as such, each has a divine nature and destiny. Gender is an essential characteristic of individual premortal, mortal, and eternal identity and purpose.

"In the premortal realm, spirit sons and daughters knew and worshiped God as their Eternal Father and accepted His plan by which His children could obtain a physical body and gain earthly experience to progress toward perfection and ultimately realize his or her divine destiny as an heir of eternal life. [Heavenly Father's great] plan of happiness enables family relationships to be perpetuated beyond the grave. Sacred ordinances and covenants available in holy temples make it possible for individuals to return to the presence of God and for families to be united eternally."[4]

The proclamation on the family helps us realize that celestial marriage brings greater possibilities for happiness than does any other relationship.⁵ The earth was created and this Church was restored so that families could be formed, sealed, and exalted eternally.⁶

Scripture declares that "it is lawful that [a man] should have one wife, and they twain shall be one flesh, and all this that the earth might answer the end of its creation" (D&C 49:16; see also Genesis 2:24; Matthew 19:5; Mark 10:7–9; D&C 42:22; Moses 3:24; Abraham 5:18). Another verse affirms that "the man [is not] without the woman, neither the woman without the man, in the Lord" (1 Corinthians 11:11). Thus, marriage is not only an exalting principle of the gospel but also a divine commandment.

Our Heavenly Father declared, "This is my work and my glory—to bring to pass the immortality and eternal life of man" (Moses 1:39). The Atonement of His Beloved Son enabled both of these objectives to be realized. Because of the Atonement, immortality—or resurrection from the dead—became a reality for all (2 Nephi 9:22; Alma 12:8; 33:22; Helaman 14:17; Mormon 9:13; Moses 7:62; JST, Genesis 7:69). And because of the Atonement, eternal life—which is living forever in God's presence, the "greatest of all the gifts of God" (D&C 14:7)—became a possibility. To qualify for eternal life, we must make an eternal and everlasting covenant with our Heavenly Father (D&C 132:19). This means that a temple marriage is not only between husband and wife; it also embraces a partnership with God (Matthew 19:6).

The proclamation on the family also reminds us that "husband and wife have a solemn responsibility to love and care for each other."⁷ Children born of that union are "an heritage of the Lord" (Psalm 127:3). When a family is sealed in the temple, that family may become as eternal as the kingdom of God itself (D&C 132:19–20).

Such a reward requires more than a hopeful wish. On occasion I read in a newspaper obituary of an expectation that a recent death has reunited that person with a deceased spouse, when, in fact, they did *not* choose the eternal option. Instead, they opted for a marriage that was valid only as long as they both should live. Heavenly Father had offered them a supernal gift, but they refused it. And in rejecting the gift, they rejected the Giver of the gift (D&C 88:33).

One strong sentence of scripture clearly distinguishes between a hopeful wish and eternal truth: "All covenants, contracts, . . . obligations, oaths, vows, . . . or expectations, that are *not* made and entered into and sealed by the Holy Spirit of promise, of him who is anointed, both as well for time and for all eternity, . . . are of *no* efficacy, virtue, or force in and after the resurrection from the dead; for all contracts that are *not* made unto this end have an end when men are dead" (D&C 132:7; emphasis added).

These truths are absolute. We who are members of the restored Church of Jesus Christ invite all people to learn them and to qualify for eternal life.[8] We invite all to gain faith in God the Eternal Father and in His Son, Jesus Christ, to repent, to receive the Holy Ghost, to obtain the blessings of the temple, to make and keep sacred covenants, and to endure to the end.

Mercifully, God's great plan of happiness and its eternal blessings can be extended to those who did not have the opportunity to hear the gospel in mortality. Temple ordinances can be done vicariously for them (D&C 128:1–18; 137:7–8).

But what of the many mature members of the Church who are not married? Through no failing of their own, they deal with the trials of life alone. Be we all reminded that, in the Lord's own way and time, no blessings will be withheld from His faithful Saints.[9] The Lord will judge and reward each individual according to heartfelt desire as well as deed (Alma 41:3; D&C 137:9).

Meanwhile, mortal misunderstandings can make mischief in a marriage. In fact, each marriage starts with two built-in handicaps. It involves two imperfect people. Happiness can come to them only through their earnest effort. Just as harmony comes from an orchestra only when its members make a concerted effort, so harmony in marriage also requires a concerted effort. That effort will succeed if each partner will minimize personal demands and maximize actions of loving selflessness.

President Thomas S. Monson has said, "To find real happiness, we must seek for it in a focus outside ourselves. No one has learned the meaning of living until he has surrendered his ego to the service of his fellow man. Service to others is akin to duty—the fulfillment of which brings true joy."[10]

Harmony in marriage comes only when each spouse esteems the welfare of the other spouse among the highest of priorities. When that happens, a celestial marriage becomes a reality, bringing great joy in this life and in the life to come.

God's plan of happiness allows us to choose for ourselves. As with the patterns of the shopper, we may choose celestial marriage or lesser alternatives (2 Nephi 2:27; Jacob 6:8). Some marital options are cheap, some are costly, and some are cunningly crafted by the adversary. Beware of his options; they always breed misery![11]

The best choice is a celestial marriage. Thankfully, if a lesser choice has previously been made, a choice can now be made to upgrade it to the best choice. That requires a mighty change of heart (Alma 5:12–14)[12] and a permanent personal upgrade.[13] Blessings so derived are worth all efforts made (D&C 93:1).

The full realization of the blessings of a temple marriage is almost beyond our mortal comprehension. Such a marriage will continue to grow in the celestial realm. There we can become perfected (Moroni 10:32). As Jesus ultimately received the fulness of the glory of the Father (D&C 93:13–14), so we may "come unto the Father . . . and in due time receive of his fulness" (D&C 93:19; see also D&C 66:2; 132:5–6).

Celestial marriage is a pivotal part of preparation for eternal life. It requires that we marry the right person in the right place by the right authority, and to obey that sacred covenant faithfully.[14] Then we may be assured of exaltation in the celestial kingdom of God.

NOTES

From a talk given at general conference, October 2008.

1. See Russell M. Nelson, "Salvation and Exaltation," *Ensign*, May 2008, 7–10.
2. One example of this objective is the scriptural declaration that "thy duty is unto the church forever, and this *because of* thy family" (D&C 23:3; emphasis added).
3. "The Family: A Proclamation to the World," *Ensign*, November 1995, 102, paragraph one.
4. "The Family: A Proclamation to the World," 102, paragraphs two and three.
5. Previously I stated that "marriage is the foundry for social order, the fountain of virtue, and the foundation for eternal exaltation" ("Nurturing Marriage," *Ensign*, May 2006, 36).
6. Whenever scriptures warn that the "earth would be utterly wasted," the warning is connected to the need for priesthood authority to seal families together in holy temples (D&C 2:1–3; 138:48; Joseph Smith—History 1:38–39).
7. "The Family: A Proclamation to the World," 102, paragraph six.
8. Jesus taught this concept to the people of ancient America (3 Nephi 27:16–20; see also 2 Nephi 33:4; D&C 42:61; JST, 1 John 5:13).
9. See Joseph Fielding Smith, *Doctrines of Salvation*, comp. Bruce R. McConkie, 3 vols. (Salt Lake City: Bookcraft, 1954–56), 2:76–77.

10. "Messages of Inspiration from President Monson," *Church News,* July 5, 2008, 2.

11. Satan wants us to be miserable, as he is (Revelation 12:9; 2 Nephi 2:18; D&C 10:22–27; Moses 4:6).

12. Such a mighty change includes repentance, forgiveness, and a renewed determination to "come unto Christ, and be perfected in him" (Moroni 10:32).

13. "The first principles and ordinances of the Gospel are: first, Faith in the Lord Jesus Christ; second, Repentance; third, Baptism by immersion for the remission of sins; fourth, Laying on of hands for the gift of the Holy Ghost" (Articles of Faith 1:4). Repentance requires a complete change for the better—a total personal upgrade.

14. See Bruce R. McConkie, *Mormon Doctrine,* 2nd ed. (Salt Lake City: Bookcraft, 1966), 118.

6

The Family:
The Hope for the Future
of Nations

As do you, I care deeply about the family. Not only do I care deeply about the worth of the family to God and to all of God's children, but I have experienced the strength that comes into the lives of a man and woman who cherish each other as husband and wife and who love their children.

My deceased wife, Dantzel, and I were blessed with nine daughters and a son. Our great joys of family life are real; our sorrows have been heart-wrenching. I know what it is to lose a daughter from cancer and to walk from her funeral carrying her two young sons in my arms. I have also felt the joy when our son-in-law married a wonderful woman who once again completed their family circle.

I know what it is to see a daughter suffer through a divorce. I have seen the pain and upheaval that ensued, and have also been grateful for the remarkable man she later married, who has again completed that family circle.

After fifty-nine years of marriage, my dear wife, Dantzel, died of a sudden rhythm shift of the heart. Ironically, my professional life as a heart surgeon included intensive research in the very malady that claimed her life. Even so, I could not resuscitate her. I know about a widower's silent loneliness.

I also know what it is to be blessed again by my Heavenly Father in marrying a second time, also to a woman of compassion and generosity of spirit, who has once again completed my family circle. Nothing, absolutely nothing, compares with the companionship between a husband and a wife. And nothing, absolutely nothing, can provide the joy and growth that come from happy children who make a family circle. Throughout my life, I have answered to many titles, including doctor, captain, professor, and elder. But the titles I revere most are those of husband, father, and grandfather.

On all sides, the family is under attack. Many wonder if the institution is no longer needed. Our response is certain: If there is any hope for the future of nations, that hope resides in the family. Our children are our wealth; our children are our strength; our children are indeed our future!

You are likely well aware of the ominous statistics. In the past fifty years, the birthrate has dropped in every nation of the world. In the nations of Europe the birthrate has dropped from the replacement rate of 2.1 children per woman to the present rate of 1.5.[1] Nations that cannot maintain their populations could even disappear, along with their culture and heritage.

Data from the United States show similar worrisome trends. In 1960, minor children formed half of the population; now they constitute only 30 percent.[2] Predictions are that by the year 2025, single-person households will outnumber families with children.[3]

What would happen to the future of nations if the next generation failed to appear in significant numbers? The answer is alarming! Yes, we would be poorer economically, but even poorer spiritually.

Spiritual concerns are of great importance. Spiritually, we need children as much as they need us. They are our spiritual wealth. Children teach us the joy of building goodness that will outlive our own. They teach us the joy of loving someone more than self. That love lifts us to give from the abundance of our own lives to help a child. I know what it is to see my dear sister, Enid, donate a kidney for her daughter, Sally, otherwise doomed to an early demise. Now, sixteen years later, they are emotionally closer and stronger, physically and spiritually.

In the twilight of life—in the golden years that can be so difficult—those individuals who made an earlier self-centered choice not to have children will be alone and unloved. They missed the point of the Psalmist who said: "As arrows are in the hand of a mighty man; so are children of the youth. Happy is the man that hath his quiver full of them" (Psalm 127:4–5).

Future happiness and even the future of nations are linked to children. Families with children need to be re-enthroned as the fundamental unit of society. We simply must value children more than we do! Without a new generation to replace the old, there is no wealth; without families, there is no future.

Children come from the union of a man and a woman. The happiest and most secure children come from happy and secure marriages of fathers and mothers. History and contemporary studies have shown that marriage of a husband and a wife, with both contributing their distinctive natural traits to the family, provides the ideal context within which to rear productive, compassionate, and moral individuals.[4]

In 2006, the parliament of France courageously rejected same-gender marriage precisely so that children would not "suffer as a result of situations imposed on them by adults. The interest of the child must outweigh the exercise of freedom by adults . . . whatever life choices are made by the parents."[5]

Any attempt to broaden the definition of marriage to encompass a contractual relationship between adults outside of the traditional family weakens the institution of marriage as God Himself defined it, and undermines the separate, divinely decreed responsibilities of man and woman for procreation, protection, and rearing of children.

Marriage is not simply a contract between individuals; it affects all of society. For that reason, governments have long recognized the family as the fundamental unit of society and have endorsed and encouraged traditional marriage through legal recognitions, protections, and benefits.

Individuals and groups who would overthrow the traditional concept of marriage and family would first mutate and then mutilate these long-established, time-tested social norms. The consequences of such changes would have far-reaching implications. If youth were to harbor the belief that the traditional family is but one choice of lifestyle among others, many of them will make choices that will reap only emptiness and despair, both for themselves and for society at large.

Furthermore, those who seek to undermine traditional marriage and family would effectively limit the rights of those who do uphold the sanctity of these institutions. This consequence leads to another major concern—the eventual erosion of religious liberty, including the liberty to defend, promote, and practice traditional family values.[6] Religious liberty is essential if we are to raise up righteous children. Morally responsible families will not marginalize religious liberty, they will nurture and protect it.

Caring people everywhere can help with persuasive statements and continuing efforts to defend marriage and promote the interests of children in traditional families. While competing voices battle for approval, our message must be clear. We can learn from Paul, who said: "There are . . . so many kinds of voices in the world, and none of them is without signification" (1 Corinthians 14:10).

"For if the trumpet give an uncertain sound, who shall prepare himself to the battle?" (1 Corinthians 14:8).

Our message is certain! Children are the hope for the future of our nations!

NOTES

From a talk given at the World Congress on Families V, Amsterdam, The Netherlands, August 2009.

1. *United Nations World Population Prospects: 2006 revision*—Table A.15n.
2. David P. Goldman, "Demographics & Depression," *First Things,* May 2009, 24.
3. Ibid.
4. This conclusion reflects what the *New York Times* has called a "powerful consensus among social scientists that 'from a child's point of view . . . the most supportive household is one with two biological parents in a low-conflict marriage.'" Hardin, *2-Parent Families Rise After Change in Welfare Laws,* quoted in *What Next for the Marriage Movement?* (New York: Institute for American Values), posted to MarriageMovement.org, 12 Dec. 2004.
5. *Report of the Mission of Inquiry on the Family and the Rights of Children,* a study commission appointed by the National Assembly of France, January 25, 2006, 46 (English translation of commission report).
6. In countries where same-gender marriage is adopted with no religious exemptions, all religions could eventually be required to perform homosexual marriages or to accept homosexual priests—even when that violates their most basic doctrines.

Doctrines
of the Kingdom

7

The Creation

The process of construction is truly inspiring to me. From conception to completion, any major building project reflects the work of the Master Creator. In fact, the Creation—of planet Earth and of life upon it—undergirds all other creative capability. Any man-made creation is possible only because of our divine Creator. The people who design and build are given life and capacity by that Creator. And all materials used in the construction of an edifice are ultimately derived from the rich resources of the earth. The Lord declared, "The earth is full, and there is enough and to spare; yea, I prepared all things" (D&C 104:17).

It is difficult for mortal minds to comprehend the majesty of the Creation. It is much easier for us to think about good things to eat or fun things to do. But I would like to stretch our minds to think of things beyond our easy grasp. The creation of man and woman was wondrous and great.[1] So was the creation of the earth as their mortal dwelling place.

The entire Creation was planned by God. A council in heaven was once convened in which we participated.[2] There our Heavenly Father announced His divine plan (2 Nephi 9:13; Alma 34:9; Abraham 3:22–27). It is also called the plan of happiness (Alma 42:8, 16), the plan of salvation (Jarom 1:2; Alma 24:14; 42:5; Moses 6:62), the plan of redemption (Jacob 6:8; Alma 12:25–34; 17:16; 18:39; 22:13; 29:2; 34:16, 31; 39:18; 42:11–13), the plan of restoration (Alma 41:2), the plan of mercy (Alma 42:15, 31; 2 Nephi 9:6), the plan of deliverance (2 Nephi 11:5), and the everlasting gospel (Revelation 14:6; D&C 27:5; 36:5; 68:1; 77:8–9, 11; 79:1; 84:103; 99:1; 101:22, 39; 106:2; 109:29, 65; 124:88; 128:17; 133:36; 135:3, 7; 138:19, 25; JS—H 1:34). The purpose of the plan is to provide opportunity for the spirit children of God to progress toward eternal exaltation.

Components of the Plan

The plan required the Creation, and that in turn required both the Fall and the Atonement. These are the three fundamental components of the plan. The creation of a paradisiacal planet came from God, and mortality and death came into the world through the Fall of Adam (2 Nephi 2:25; Moses 6:48; JST, Genesis 6:49). Immortality and the possibility of eternal life came through the Atonement of Jesus Christ (2 Nephi 2:21–28). The Creation, the Fall, and the Atonement were planned long before the actual work of the Creation began.

While visiting the British Museum in London one day, I read a most unusual book. It is not scripture. It is an English translation of an ancient Egyptian manuscript. From it, I quote a dialogue between the Father and the Son. Referring to His Father, Jehovah—the premortal Lord—says:

"He took the clay from the hand of the angel, and made Adam according to Our image and likeness, and He left him lying for forty days and forty nights without putting breath into him. And He heaved sighs over him daily, saying, 'If I put breath into this [man], he must suffer many pains.' And I said unto My Father, 'Put breath into him; I will be an advocate for him.' And My Father said unto Me, 'If I put breath into him, My beloved Son, Thou wilt be obliged to go down into the world, and to suffer many pains for him before Thou shalt have redeemed him, and made him to come back to his primal state.' And I said unto My Father, 'Put breath into him; I will be his advocate, and I will go down into the world, and will fulfil Thy command.'"[3]

Although this text is not scripture, it reaffirms scriptures that teach of the deep and compassionate love of the Father for the Son, and of the Son for us—attesting that Jesus volunteered willingly to be our Savior and Redeemer (John 3:16; 10:14–15, 17–18).

The Lord God declared, "This is my work and my glory—to bring to pass the immortality and eternal life of man" (Moses 1:39). He who, under the direction of the Father, had created the earth subsequently came into mortality to do the will of His Father (3 Nephi 27:13) and to fulfill all prophecies of the Atonement.[4] His Atonement would redeem every soul from the penalties of personal transgression on conditions that He set (2 Nephi 9:20–27; Mosiah 26:21–23; D&C 138:19).

Phases of the Creation

Each phase of the Creation was well planned before it was accomplished. Scripture tells us that "the Lord God, created all things . . . spiritually, before they were naturally upon the face of the earth" (Moses 3:5; 6:51).

The physical Creation itself was staged through ordered periods of time. In Genesis (vv. 1:5–2:3) and Moses (vv. 2:5–3:3), those periods are called *days.* But in the book of Abraham, each period is referred to as a *time* (vv. 4:5–5:3). Whether termed a *day,* a *time,* or an *age,* each phase was a period between two identifiable events—a division of eternity.[5]

Period one included the creation of atmospheric heavens and physical earth, culminating in the emergence of light from darkness (Genesis 1:1–5; Moses 2:1–5; Abraham 4:1–5).

In period two, the waters were divided between the surface of the earth and its atmospheric heavens. Provision was made for clouds and rain to give life to all that would later dwell upon the earth (Genesis 1:6–8; Moses 2:6–8; Abraham 4:6–8).

In period three, plant life began. The earth was organized to bring forth grass, herbs, trees, and vegetation—each growing from its own seed (Genesis 1:9–13; Moses 2:9–13; Abraham 4:9–13).

Period four was a time of further development. Lights in the expanse of the heavens were organized so there could be seasons and other means of measuring time. During this period, the sun, the moon, the stars, and the earth were placed in proper relationship to one another (Genesis 1:14–19; Moses 2:14–19; Abraham 4:14–19). The sun, with its vast stores of hydrogen, was to serve as a giant furnace to provide light and heat for the earth and life upon it.[6]

In period five, fish, fowl, and "every living creature" were added (Abraham 4:20–21). They were made fruitful and able to multiply—in the sea and on the earth—each after its own kind (Genesis 1:20–23; Moses 2:20–23; Abraham 4:22–23).

In the sixth period, creation of life continued. The beasts of the earth were made after their kind, cattle after their kind, and everything that "creepeth upon the earth"—again, after its own kind (Genesis 1:24–31; Moses 2:24–31; Abraham 4:24–31).

Then the Gods counseled together and said: "Let us go down and form man in our image, after our likeness. . . . So the Gods went down to organize man in their own image, in the image of the Gods to form they him, male and female to form they them" (Abraham 4:26–27). Thus, Adam and Eve were formed.[7] And they were blessed to "be fruitful, and multiply, and replenish the earth, and subdue it: and have dominion over the fish of the sea, and over the fowl of the air, and over every living thing that moveth upon the earth" (Genesis 1:28; Moses 2:28; see also Abraham 4:28; JST, Genesis 1:30).

The seventh period, designated as a time of rest, then followed (Genesis 2:1–3; Moses 3:1–3; Abraham 5:1–3).

The Creation Testifies of a Creator

I testify that the earth and all life upon it are of divine origin. The Creation did not happen by chance. It did not come *ex nihilo* (out of nothing). And human minds and hands able to build buildings or create computers are not accidental. It is God who made us and not we ourselves. We are His people! (Psalm 100:3). The Creation itself testifies of a Creator. We cannot disregard the divine in the Creation. Without our grateful awareness of God's hand in the Creation, we would be just as oblivious to our provider as are goldfish swimming in a bowl.

With deep gratitude, we echo the words of the Psalmist, who said, "O Lord, how manifold are thy works! in wisdom hast thou made them all: the earth is full of thy riches" (Psalm 104:24).

Purpose and Destiny of the Earth

This earth is but one of many creations over which God presides. "Worlds without number have I created," He said. "And I also created them for mine own purpose; and by the Son I created them, which is mine Only Begotten" (Moses 1:33; see also D&C 76:23–24). Grand as it is, planet Earth is part of something even grander—that great plan of God. Simply summarized, the earth was created that families might be. Scripture explains that a husband and wife "shall be one flesh, and all this that the earth might answer the end of its creation" (D&C 49:16).

And as part of the planned destiny of the earth and its inhabitants, here our kindred dead are also to be redeemed (D&C 128:15). Families are to be sealed together for all eternity (D&C 2:2–3; 49:17; 138:48; JS—H 1:39). A welding link is to be forged between the fathers and the children. In our time, a whole, complete, and perfect union of all dispensations, keys, and powers are to be welded together (D&C 128:18). For these sacred purposes, holy temples now dot the earth.

Though our understanding of the Creation is limited, we know enough to appreciate its supernal significance. And that store of knowledge will be augmented in the future. Scripture declares:

"In that day when the Lord shall come [again], he shall reveal all things—things which have passed, and hidden things which no man knew, things of the earth, by which it was made, and the purpose and the end thereof—things most precious, things that are above, and things that are beneath, things that are in the earth, and upon the earth, and in heaven" (D&C 101:32–34).

Yes, further light and knowledge will come. The Lord said, "If there be bounds set to the heavens or to the seas, or to the dry land, or to the sun, moon, or stars—all the times of their revolutions, all the appointed days, months, and years, . . . and all their glories, laws, and set times, shall be revealed in the days of the dispensation of the fulness of times" (D&C 121:30–31).

Eventually, "the earth will be renewed and receive its paradisiacal glory" (Articles of Faith 1:10). At the Second Coming of the Lord, the earth will be changed once again. It will be returned to its paradisiacal state and be made new. There will be a new heaven and a new earth (Revelation 21:1; Ether 13:9; D&C 29:23–24).

Our Responsibilities

Meanwhile, we should understand our significant responsibilities. Both the creations of God and the creations of man teach us the importance of each component. Do you think that the absence of one piece of granite from the face of the Church's Conference Center would be noticed? Of course it would!

So it is with each son or daughter of God. We cannot let "the head say unto the feet it [has] no need of the feet; for without the feet how shall the body be able to stand?" (D&C 84:109). Just as "the body [has] need of every member" (D&C 84:110), so the family has need of every member. All members of a family are to be linked, sealed, and "edified together, that the system may be kept perfect" (D&C 84:110; see also 1 Corinthians 12:14–26).

The Creation, great as it is, is not an end in itself but a means to an end. We come to the earth for a brief period of time, endure our tests and trials, and prepare to move onward and upward to a glorious homecoming (Psalm 116:15; Alma 42:8). Our thoughts and deeds while here will surely be more purposeful if we understand God's plan and are thankful for and obedient to His commandments (D&C 59:20–21).

As beneficiaries of the divine Creation, what should we do? We should care for the earth, be wise stewards over it, and preserve it for future generations.[8] And we are to love and care for one another (John 13:34–35; 15:12; Romans 12:10–13:8; Galatians 5:13; 1 Thessalonians 4:9; 1 John 3:11; 4:12; Mosiah 4:15; D&C 88:123).

We are to be creators in our own right—builders of an individual faith in God, faith in the Lord Jesus Christ, and faith in His Church. We are to build families and be sealed in holy temples. We are to build the Church and kingdom of God upon the earth (JST, Matthew 6:38; see also KJV, Matthew 6:33 note a). We are to prepare for our own divine destiny— glory, immortality, and eternal lives (Romans 2:7; D&C 75:5; 128:12; 132:19–24). These supernal blessings can all be ours through our faithfulness.

NOTES

From a talk given at general conference, April 2000.

1. See Russell M. Nelson, "The Magnificence of Man," *Ensign,* January 1988, 64–69; "We Are Children of God," *Ensign,* November 1998, 85–87.

2. See *Teachings of the Prophet Joseph Smith,* sel. Joseph Fielding Smith (Salt Lake City: Deseret Book, 1976), 349–50, 365.

3. "Discourse on Abbatôn by Timothy, Archbishop of Alexandria," in *Coptic Martyrdoms, etc., in the Dialect of Upper Egypt,* ed. and trans. E. A. Wallis Budge (London: British Museum, 1914), 482. Timothy, Archbishop of Alexandria, died in A.D. 385. Brackets are included in Budge's English translation.

4. For a comprehensive study of the prophecies of prophets pertaining to Christ, see D. Kelly Ogden and R. Val Johnson, "All the Prophets Prophesied of Christ," *Ensign,* January 1994, 31–37.

5. Abraham likened one day in the Lord's time to one thousand years (Abraham 3:4).

6. See Henry Eyring, "World of Evidence, World of Faith," in *Of Heaven and Earth: Reconciling Scientific Thought with LDS Theology,* ed. David L. Clark (Salt Lake City: Deseret Book, 1998), 59.

7. Note that the Lord called the first man *and* woman "Adam" (Genesis 5:2; Moses 6:9).

8. The Lord has entrusted us to care for the earth. He said, "It is expedient that I, the Lord, should make every man accountable, as a steward over earthly blessings, which I have made and prepared for my creatures. I, the Lord, stretched out the heavens, and built the earth, my very handiwork; and all things therein are mine. And it is my purpose to provide for my saints, for all things are mine" (D&C 104:13–15; see also Revelation 7:3).

8

Jesus Christ—
The Master Healer

I express special gratitude to the Lord Jesus Christ. I am thankful for His loving-kindness and for His open invitation to come unto Him (Matthew 11:28–30).[1] I marvel at His matchless power to heal. I testify of Jesus Christ as the Master Healer. It is but one of many attributes that characterize His incomparable life.

Jesus is the Christ, the Messiah, the Son of God, the Creator, the great Jehovah, the promised Immanuel, our atoning Savior and Redeemer, our Advocate with the Father, our great Exemplar. And one day we will stand before Him as our just and merciful Judge.[2]

Miracles of Healing

As the Master Healer, Jesus directed His friends to "go . . . and tell . . . what things ye have seen and heard; how that the blind see, the lame walk, the lepers are cleansed, the deaf hear, [and] the dead are raised" (Luke 7:22).

The books of Matthew (Matthew 4:23; 8:1–3, 5–13, 16–17; 9:1–8, 32–35; 12:15; 14:14, 34–36; 15:29–31), Mark (Mark 1:32–34, 40–45; 2:1–12; 6:53–56; 7:31–37), Luke (Luke 4:40–41; 5:12–15, 17–26; 7:1–10; 11:14; 22:50–51), and John (John 4:46–53) repeatedly report that Jesus went about preaching the gospel and healing all types of sickness.

When the risen Redeemer appeared to the people of ancient America, He mercifully invited those "afflicted in any manner" (3 Nephi 17:7) to come unto Him and be healed.

Marvelously, His divine authority to heal the sick was conferred upon worthy priesthood bearers in earlier dispensations (Matthew 10:5–8; Mark 16:17; Luke 10:17; 4 Nephi 1:5) and again in these latter days, when His gospel has been restored in its fulness (D&C 84:65–70).

Influence of Prayer on Healing

We can also access His healing power through prayer. I'll never forget an experience that Sister Nelson and I had about three decades ago with President Spencer W. Kimball and his beloved Camilla. We were in Hamilton, New Zealand, for a large conference with the Saints. I was not a General Authority at that time. I had been invited to participate in this and similar meetings in other Pacific islands while serving as general president of the Sunday School. And as a doctor of medicine, I had attended President and Sister Kimball for many years. I knew each of them very well—inside and out.

A Saturday evening cultural program had been prepared for this conference by local youth of the Church. Unfortunately,

President and Sister Kimball both became very ill, each with a high fever. After receiving priesthood blessings, they rested at the nearby home of the president of the New Zealand Temple. President Kimball asked one of his counselors, President N. Eldon Tanner, to preside at the cultural event and to excuse him and Sister Kimball.

Sister Nelson went with President and Sister Tanner and other leaders to the event, while President Kimball's secretary, Brother D. Arthur Haycock, and I watched over our feverish friends.

While President Kimball was sleeping, I was quietly reading in his room. Suddenly President Kimball awakened. He asked, "Brother Nelson, what time was this evening's program to begin?"

"At seven o'clock, President Kimball."

"What time is it now?"

"It's almost seven," I replied.

President Kimball quickly said, "Tell Sister Kimball we are going!"

I checked President Kimball's temperature. It was normal! I took Sister Kimball's temperature. It was also normal!

They quickly dressed and got into an automobile. We were driven to the stadium of the Church College of New Zealand. As the car entered the arena, a very loud shout erupted spontaneously. It was most unusual! After we took our seats, I asked Sister Nelson about that sudden sound. She said that when President Tanner began the meeting, he dutifully excused President and Sister Kimball because of illness. Then one of the young New Zealanders was called upon to pray.

With great faith, he gave what Sister Nelson described as a rather lengthy but powerful prayer. He prayed: "We are three thousand New Zealand youth. We are assembled here, having prepared for six months to sing and dance for Thy prophet. Wilt Thou heal him and deliver him here!" After the "amen" was pronounced, the car carrying President and Sister Kimball entered the stadium. They were identified immediately, and instantly everyone shouted for joy![3]

I had witnessed the healing power of the Lord! I had also witnessed revelation as received and responded to by His living prophet!

I recognize that, on occasion, some of our most fervent prayers may seem to go unanswered. We wonder, "Why?" I know that feeling! I know the fears and tears of such moments. But I also know that our prayers are never ignored. Our faith is never unappreciated. I know that an all-wise Heavenly Father's perspective is much broader than is ours. While we know of our mortal problems and pain, He knows of our immortal progress and potential. If we pray to know His will and submit ourselves to it with patience and courage, heavenly healing can take place in His own way and time.

Steps toward Healing

Afflictions can come from spiritual as well as physical causes. Alma the Younger remembered that his sin was so painful that he wished to "become extinct both soul and body, that [he] might not be brought to stand in the presence of . . . God, to be judged of [his] deeds" (Alma 36:15). At such times, how can we be healed by Him?

We can more fully repent! We can become more fully converted! Then the "Son of Righteousness" (3 Nephi 25:2; see also Malachi 4:2) can more fully bless us by His healing hand.

Early in His mortal ministry, Jesus announced that He had

been sent "to heal the brokenhearted" (Luke 4:18; see also Isaiah 61:1). Wherever He taught, His pattern was consistent. As I cite His words spoken at four different times and locations, note the pattern.

To people of the Holy Land, the Lord said that His people "should see with their eyes, and hear with their ears, and should understand with their heart, and should be converted, and I should heal them" (Matthew 13:15; see also Isaiah 6:10; John 12:40; Acts 28:27).

To people of ancient America, the resurrected Lord extended this invitation: "Return unto me, . . . repent of your sins, and be converted, that I may heal you" (3 Nephi 9:13).

To leaders of His Church, He taught, "Continue to minister; for ye know not but what they will return and repent, and come unto me with full purpose of heart, and I shall heal them" (3 Nephi 18:32).

Later, during the "restitution of all things" (Acts 3:21), the Lord taught the Prophet Joseph Smith regarding the trials the Saints would face: "After their temptations, and much tribulation, behold, I, the Lord, will feel after them, and if they harden not their hearts, and stiffen not their necks against me, they shall be converted, and I will heal them" (D&C 112:13; see also D&C 124:104).

The sequence of His pattern is significant. Faith, repentance, baptism, a testimony, and enduring conversion lead to the healing power of the Lord. Baptism is a covenant act—a sign of a commitment and a promise. Testimony develops when the Holy Ghost gives conviction to the earnest seeker of the truth. True testimony fosters faith; it promotes repentance and obedience to God's commandments. Testimony engenders enthusiasm to serve God and fellow human beings.[4] Conversion means "to turn with."[5] Conversion is a turning *from* the ways of the world *to,* and staying *with,* the ways of the Lord. Conversion includes repentance and obedience. Conversion brings a mighty change of heart (Mosiah 5:2; Alma 5:12–14). Thus, a true convert is "born again" (John 3:3–7; 1 Peter 1:23; Mosiah 27:24–26; Alma 5:49; 7:14; Moses 6:59; JST, Genesis 6:62), walking with a newness of life (Romans 6:3–4).

As true converts, we are motivated to do what the Lord wants us to do (Mosiah 5:2–5) and to be who He wants us to be (3 Nephi 27:21, 27). The remission of sins, which brings divine forgiveness, heals the spirit.

How do we know if we are truly converted? Self-examination tests are available in the scriptures. One measures the degree of conversion prerequisite to baptism (D&C 20:37; Mosiah 18:10). Another measures our willingness to serve others. To His disciple Peter, the Lord said, "I have prayed for thee, that thy faith fail not: and when thou art converted, strengthen thy brethren" (Luke 22:32). Willingness to serve and strengthen others stands as a symbol of our readiness to be healed.

Magnitude of His Healing

John the Beloved declared, "Behold the Lamb of God, who taketh away the sin of the world!" (JST, John 1:29). What power! Only the Master Healer could take away the sin of the world. Our debt to Him is incalculably great.

Well do I remember an experience while speaking to a group of missionaries. After I had invited questions, one elder stood. With tears in his eyes, he asked, "Why did Jesus have to suffer so much?" I asked the elder to open his hymnbook and recite words from "How Great Thou Art." He read:

And when I think that God, his Son not sparing,
Sent him to die, I scarce can take it in,
That on the cross, my burden gladly bearing,
He bled and died to take away my sin.[6]

Then I asked this elder to read from "Reverently and Meekly Now." These words are particularly poignant because they are written as if the Lord had expressed His own answer to the *very* question the missionary had asked:

Think of me, thou ransomed one;
Think what I for thee have done.
With my blood that dripped like rain,
Sweat in agony of pain,
With my body on the tree
I have ransomed even thee. . . .
Oh, remember what was done
That the sinner might be won.
On the cross of Calvary
I have suffered death for thee.[7]

Jesus suffered deeply because He loves us deeply! He wants us to repent and be converted so that He can fully heal us.

When sore trials come upon us,[8] it's time to deepen our faith in God, to work hard, and to serve others. Then He will heal our broken hearts. He will bestow upon us personal peace (John 14:27) and comfort (Isaiah 40:1; John 14:16–17, 26). Those great gifts will not be destroyed, even by death.

Resurrection—the Consummate Act of Healing

The gift of resurrection is the Lord's consummate act of healing. Thanks to Him, each body will be restored to its proper and perfect frame (Alma 11:43; 40:23).

Thanks to Him, no condition is hopeless. Thanks to Him, brighter days are ahead, both here and hereafter. Real joy awaits each of us—on the other side of sorrow.

NOTES

From a talk given at general conference, October 2005.

1. Indeed, His yoke is easy and His burden is light.
2. See Russell M. Nelson, "Jesus the Christ, Our Master and More," *Ensign*, April 2000, 4–17.
3. Spencer J. Condie, *Russell M. Nelson: Father, Surgeon, Apostle* (Salt Lake City: Deseret Book, 2003), 172–74.
4. Testimony helps us keep the two great commandments: "Thou shalt love the Lord thy God with all thy heart, and with all thy soul, and with all thy strength, and with all thy mind; and thy neighbour as thyself" (Luke 10:27).
5. *Conversion* comes from two Latin roots: *con*, meaning "with," and *vertere*, meaning "to turn."
6. *Hymns* (Salt Lake City: The Church of Jesus Christ of Latter-day Saints, 1985), no. 86; see also Psalms 8:3–9; 9:1–2; Mosiah 4:5–13.
7. *Hymns*, no. 185; see also D&C 19:16–19; 45:3–5.
8. See "Did You Think to Pray?" *Hymns*, no. 140, verse 3.

9

The Gathering of
Scattered Israel

We share an enormous responsibility to be who the Lord wants us to be and to do what He wants us to do. We are part of a great movement—the gathering of scattered Israel. I speak of this doctrine because of its unique importance in God's eternal plan.

The Abrahamic Covenant

Anciently, the Lord blessed Father Abraham with a promise to make his posterity a chosen people (Genesis 12:1–2; D&C 132:29–32; Abraham 2:6–11). References to this covenant occur throughout the scriptures. Included were promises that the Son of God would come through Abraham's lineage, that certain lands would be inherited, that nations and kindreds of the earth would be blessed through his seed, and more (Genesis 26:1–4, 24, 28; 35:9–13; 48:3–4; John 8:33, 39; Acts 3:25; 1 Nephi 17:40; 2 Nephi 29:14; Jacob 5; Ether 13:7–8; D&C 52:2). While some aspects of this covenant have already been fulfilled, the Book of Mormon teaches that this Abrahamic covenant will be fulfilled only in these latter days! (1 Nephi 15:12–18). It also emphasizes that we are among the covenant people of the Lord (1 Nephi 14:14; 15:14; 2 Nephi 30:2; Mosiah 24:13; 3 Nephi 29:3; Mormon 8:15; D&C 133:26–34). Ours is the privilege to participate personally in the fulfillment of these promises. What an exciting time to live!

Israel Became Scattered

As descendants of Abraham, the tribes of ancient Israel had access to priesthood authority and blessings of the gospel, but eventually the people rebelled. They killed the prophets and were punished by the Lord. Ten tribes were carried captive into Assyria. From there they became lost to the records of mankind.[1] Two remaining tribes continued a short time and then, because of their rebellion, were taken captive into Babylon.[2] When they returned, they were favored of the Lord, but again they honored Him not. They rejected and vilified Him. A loving but grieving Father vowed, "I will scatter you among the heathen" (Leviticus 26:33; see also Jeremiah 9:16), and that He did—into all nations.

Israel to Be Gathered

God's promise for the gathering of scattered Israel was equally emphatic (Genesis 22:16–18; 3 Nephi 20–22; Abraham 2:10–11). Isaiah, for example, foresaw that in the latter days the

Lord would send "swift messengers" to these people who were so "scattered and peeled" (Isaiah 18:2, 7).

This promise of the gathering of Israel, woven all through the fabric of the scriptures, will be fulfilled just as surely as were the prophecies of the scattering of Israel (Leviticus 26:44; Deuteronomy 4:27–31; 28; 29; 30:2–5; Nehemiah 1:9; Isaiah 11:11–12; Jeremiah 31:7–8, 10–12; Ezekiel 37:21–22; Amos 9:14–15; Matthew 24:31; Jacob 6:2).

The Church of Jesus Christ in the Meridian of Time and the Apostasy

Prior to His Crucifixion, the Lord Jesus Christ had established His Church. It included apostles, prophets, seventies, teachers, and so forth (Luke 10:1, 17; Ephesians 4:11; Articles of Faith 1:6). In addition, the Master sent His disciples into the world to preach His gospel (Matthew 28:19–20; Mark 16:15).

After a time the Church as established by the Lord fell into spiritual decay. His teachings were altered; His ordinances were changed. The Great Apostasy came as had been foretold by Paul, who knew that the Lord would not come again "except there come a falling away first" (2 Thessalonians 2:3).[3]

This Great Apostasy followed the pattern that had ended each previous dispensation. The first was in the time of Adam. Then came the dispensations of Enoch, Noah, Abraham, Moses, and others. Each prophet had a divine commission to teach of the divinity and the doctrine of the Lord Jesus Christ. In each age these teachings were meant to help the people. But their disobedience resulted in apostasy. Thus, all previous dispensations were limited in time and location. They were limited in time because each ended in apostasy. They were limited in location to a relatively small segment of the earth.

The Restoration of All Things

Thus a complete restoration was required. God the Father and Jesus Christ called upon the Prophet Joseph Smith to be the prophet of this dispensation. All divine powers of previous dispensations were to be restored through him (D&C 128:18; 132:45). This dispensation of the fulness of times would not be limited in time or location. It would not end in apostasy, and it would fill the world (Isaiah 27:6).

The Gathering of Israel—an Integral Part of the Restoration of All Things

As prophesied by the Apostles Peter and Paul, *all* things were to be restored in this dispensation. Therefore, there must come, as part of that restoration, the long-awaited gathering of scattered Israel (1 Nephi 15:18; see also Book of Mormon title page, paragraph 2). It is a necessary prelude to the Second Coming of the Lord (D&C 133:17).

This doctrine of the gathering is one of the important teachings of The Church of Jesus Christ of Latter-day Saints. The Lord has declared, "I give unto you a sign . . . that I shall gather in, from their long dispersion, my people, O house of Israel, and shall establish again among them my Zion" (3 Nephi 21:1). The coming forth of the Book of Mormon is a sign to the entire world that the Lord has commenced to gather Israel and fulfill covenants He made to Abraham, Isaac, and Jacob

(Genesis 12:2–3; 26:3–4; 35:11–12; chapter headings for 3 Nephi 21; 29).

We not only teach this doctrine, but we also participate in it. We do so as we help to gather the elect of the Lord on both sides of the veil.

The Book of Mormon is central to this work. It declares the doctrine of the gathering.[4] It causes people to learn about Jesus Christ, to believe His gospel, and to join His Church. In fact, if there were no Book of Mormon, the promised gathering of Israel would not occur.[5]

To us the honored name of *Abraham* is important. It is mentioned in more verses of the scriptures of the Restoration than in all the verses of the Bible.[6] Abraham is linked to all members of The Church of Jesus Christ of Latter-day Saints.[7] The Lord reaffirmed the Abrahamic covenant in our day through the Prophet Joseph Smith (D&C 124:58; 132:31–32). In the temple we receive our ultimate blessings as the seed of Abraham, Isaac, and Jacob (D&C 84:33–40; 132:19; Abraham 2:11).

The Dispensation of the Fulness of Times

The dispensation of the fulness of times was foreseen by God as the time to gather, both in heaven and on earth. Peter knew that after a period of apostasy, a restoration would come. He, who had been with the Lord on the Mount of Transfiguration, declared:

"Repent ye therefore, and be converted, that your sins may be blotted out, when the times of refreshing shall come from the presence of the Lord; . . . whom the heaven must receive until the times of restitution of all things, which God hath spoken by the mouth of all his holy prophets since the world began" (Acts 3:19, 21).

In modern times the Apostles Peter, James, and John were sent by the Lord with "the keys of [His] kingdom, and a dispensation of the gospel for the last times; and for the fulness of times," in which He would "gather together in one all things, both which are in heaven, and which are on earth" (D&C 27:13).[8]

In the year 1830 the Prophet Joseph Smith learned of a heavenly messenger named Elias, who possessed keys to bring to pass "the restoration of all things" (D&C 27:6).

Six years later the Kirtland Temple was dedicated. After the Lord accepted that holy house, heavenly messengers came with priesthood keys. Moses appeared[9] "and committed . . . the keys of the gathering of Israel from the four parts of the earth, and the leading of the ten tribes from the land of the north. After this, Elias appeared, and committed the dispensation of the gospel of Abraham, saying that in us and our seed all generations after us should be blessed" (D&C 110:11–12).

Then Elijah the prophet came and proclaimed, "Behold, the time has fully come, which was spoken of by the mouth of Malachi—testifying that he [Elijah] should be sent, before the great and dreadful day of the Lord come—to turn the hearts of the fathers to the children, and the children to the fathers, lest the whole earth be smitten with a curse" (D&C 110:14–15).

These events occurred on April 3, 1836,[10] and thus fulfilled Malachi's prophecy (Malachi 4:5–6). Sacred keys of this dispensation were restored (D&C 110:16).

Gathering of Souls on the Other Side of the Veil

Mercifully, the invitation to "come unto Christ" (Jacob 1:7; Omni 1:26; Moroni 10:30, 32; D&C 20:59) can also be extended to those who died without a knowledge of the gospel (D&C 137:6–8). Part of their preparation, however, requires the earthly efforts of others. We gather pedigree charts, create family group sheets, and do temple work vicariously to gather individuals unto the Lord and into their families (1 Corinthians 15:29; 1 Peter 4:6).

To Participate in the Gathering: A Commitment by Covenant

Here on earth, missionary work is crucial to the gathering of Israel. The gospel was to be taken first to the "lost sheep of the house of Israel" (Matthew 10:6; 15:24). Consequently, servants of the Lord have gone forth proclaiming the Restoration. In many nations our missionaries have searched for those of scattered Israel; they have hunted for them "out of the holes of the rocks" (Jeremiah 16:16); and they have fished for them as in ancient days.

The choice to come unto Christ is not a matter of physical location; it is a matter of individual commitment. People can be "brought to the knowledge of the Lord" (3 Nephi 20:13) without leaving their homelands. True, in the early days of the Church, conversion often meant emigration as well. But now the gathering takes place in each nation. The Lord has decreed the establishment of Zion (D&C 6:6; 11:6; 12:6; 14:6) in each realm where He has given His Saints their birth and nationality.

Scripture foretells that the people "shall be gathered home to the lands of their inheritance, and shall be established in all their lands of promise" (2 Nephi 9:2). "Every nation is the gathering place for its own people."[11] The place of gathering for Brazilian Saints is in Brazil; the place of gathering for Nigerian Saints is in Nigeria; the place of gathering for Korean Saints is in Korea; and so forth. Zion is "the pure in heart" (D&C 97:21).

Zion is wherever righteous Saints are. Publications, communications, and congregations are now such that nearly all members of the Church have access to the doctrines, keys, ordinances, and blessings of the gospel, regardless of their location.

Spiritual security will always depend upon *how* one lives, not *where* one lives. Saints in every land have equal claim upon the blessings of the Lord.

This work of Almighty God is true. He lives. Jesus is the Christ. This is His Church, restored to accomplish its divine destiny, including the promised gathering of Israel.

NOTES

From a talk given at general conference, October 2006.

1. Obviously, the ten tribes are not lost to the Lord.
2. The tribe of Levi provided priests among the people and was not to be numbered as a tribe or to receive tribal inheritance. The two sons of Joseph, Ephraim and Manasseh, were given land inheritances. They were numbered among the tribes in the stead of their father, Joseph. The number of twelve tribes was thus maintained.
3. "Falling away" is translated from the Greek *apostasia,* meaning "apostasy."
4. Doctrines relating to the scattering and gathering of the house of Israel are among the earliest lessons taught in the Book of Mormon: "After the house of Israel should be scattered they should be gathered together again; . . . the natural branches of the olive-tree, or the remnants of the house of Israel,

should be grafted in, or come to the knowledge of the true Messiah, their Lord and their Redeemer" (1 Nephi 10:14).

5. See Bruce R. McConkie, *A New Witness for the Articles of Faith* (Salt Lake City: Deseret Book, 1985), 554.

6. Abraham is mentioned in 506 verses of scripture: 216 are in the Bible; 290 are in the scriptures of the Restoration.

7. The covenant may also be received by adoption (Matthew 3:9; Luke 3:8; Galatians 3:26–29; 4:5–7; Abraham 2:9–10).

8. Paul also prophesied of our day "that in the dispensation of the fulness of times [the Lord] might gather together in one all things in Christ, both which are in heaven, and which are on earth" (Ephesians 1:10).

9. It is appropriate that Moses, who led God's children to the land of their inheritance, would be the one to commit the keys of the gathering of Israel to the restored Church. Moses had come to Peter, James, and John on the Mount of Transfiguration and there bestowed upon them the same priesthood keys in their day. At the conference of the Church in April 1840, the Prophet Joseph Smith appointed Orson Hyde to go to Jerusalem to dedicate the land for the return of the Jews and scattered Israel. On Sunday, October 24, 1841, Elder Hyde knelt on the Mount of Olives and dedicated that land for the gathering of the Jews and of Israel to their ancient inheritance.

10. Significant is the fact that Moses, Elias, and Elijah came on Easter Sunday, at the beginning of Passover.

11. Bruce R. McConkie, in report of Mexico and Central America Area Conference, August 26, 1972, 45.

10

The Exodus Repeated

Many instructive parallels exist between the exodus from Egypt of the Israelites under Moses and the exodus from the United States of the Latter-day Saint pioneers under Brigham Young. When we honor those early converts to The Church of Jesus Christ of Latter-day Saints, we sense a deep debt of gratitude to them. But I also chose this topic because we can learn much from these stalwarts of ancient and modern Israel.

Generally, sketches and pageants have portrayed well *what* the pioneers did. But only a few writers have delved deeply enough to explain *why*. And even fewer have reported the similarities between the pioneer trek and the exodus from Egypt. That exodus was a type and shadow for the exodus of the pioneers.

An obvious likeness is that both groups had their inland sea of salt water and a River Jordan. But there were many other significant similarities. Ancient Israel and modern Israel are linked arm in arm.

The Josephs

Ancient Israel had leaders before Moses, and modern Israel had a prophet-president before Brigham Young. Predecessors for each group also bore a resemblance. A name common to both was Joseph—Joseph who was sold into Egypt and the Prophet Joseph Smith.

Few men in the Old Testament are of greater importance to Latter-day Saints than Joseph of Egypt. Many of us claim lineage from Joseph through his sons, Ephraim and Manasseh.

The Book of Mormon reveals that "a part of the remnant of the coat of Joseph was preserved and had not decayed. Even as this remnant of garment . . . hath been preserved, so shall a remnant of the seed . . . be preserved by the hand of God, and be taken unto himself" (Alma 46:24).

The pioneers were remnants of that precious seed. They knew that Joseph Smith had been chosen by the Lord to take up the labors of the tribe of Joseph, son of Jacob. Centuries earlier, Joseph had prophesied of Joseph Smith and had described their kinship:

"Yea, Joseph truly said: Thus saith the Lord unto me: A choice seer will I raise up out of the fruit of thy loins; and he shall be esteemed highly among the fruit of thy loins. And unto him will I give commandment that he shall do a work for the fruit of thy loins, his brethren, which shall be of great worth unto them, even to the bringing of them to the knowledge of the covenants which I have made with thy fathers.

"And I will give unto him a commandment that he shall do none other work, save the work which I shall command him. And I will make him great in mine eyes; for he shall do my work" (2 Nephi 3:7–8).

The name of Joseph applied not only to Joseph Smith Jr. but to his father as well. Again I quote from Joseph who was sold into Egypt:

"Behold, that seer [Joseph Smith] will the Lord bless; . . . for this promise, which I have obtained of the Lord, of the fruit of my loins, shall be fulfilled. . . . And his name shall be called after me; and it shall be after the name of his father. And he shall be like unto me; for the thing, which the Lord shall bring forth by his hand, by the power of the Lord shall bring my people unto salvation" (2 Nephi 3:14–15).[1]

Jacob's son Joseph and Joseph Smith had even more in common. At age seventeen, Joseph of old was informed of his great destiny (Genesis 37:2). At the same age, Joseph Smith was informed of his destiny regarding the Book of Mormon. At age seventeen, he was visited for the first time by the angel Moroni, who informed the boy prophet that "God had a work for [him] to do." He was to translate a book written upon golden plates containing the fulness of the everlasting gospel. His "name should be had for good and evil among all nations, kindreds, and tongues" (Joseph Smith—History 1:33; see also vv. 34–41).

Both Josephs endured persecution. Joseph of old was falsely accused of a crime he did not commit and put into prison (Genesis 39:11–20). Joseph Smith likewise suffered incarceration on trumped up charges and false accusations.[2]

Joseph's brothers betrayed him, taking from him his coat of many colors in a cruel attempt to convince their father that Joseph had been killed (Genesis 37:2–33). Joseph Smith's life was cruelly taken from him, largely because of betrayals by false brethren.

Anciently, when "all the land of Egypt was famished, the people cried to Pharaoh for bread: and Pharaoh said unto all the Egyptians, Go unto Joseph; what he saith to you, do" (Genesis 41:55). In the latter days, people starving for nourishment that only the gospel can provide are again to be fed—by Joseph. The Lord declared that "this generation shall have my word through [Joseph Smith]" (D&C 5:10). Today we may "feast upon the words of Christ" (2 Nephi 32:3) because of him.

Moses and Brigham Young

Moses and Brigham Young had much in common. They were astute followers before they became great leaders. Moses had been prepared in the courts of Egypt and had gained much experience in military and other responsibilities (Hebrews 11:24, 27). Brigham Young was likewise prepared for his leadership role. In the march of Zion's Camp, he had observed the leadership of the Prophet Joseph Smith under difficult conditions.[3] Brigham Young aided in the removal of the Saints from Kirtland.[4] He also directed the move of the persecuted Saints from Missouri to Nauvoo.[5]

For both groups, civil and ecclesiastical law were unified under one head. Moses bore that responsibility for his people.[6] Brigham Young—the modern Moses (D&C 103:16)[7]—led the Latter-day Saints' movement west, with the Lord's blessing (D&C 136:1–42). Moses and Brigham Young followed parallel patterns of governance (Exodus 18:17–21; D&C 136:1–3),

Other Old Testament passages foretell of the Book of Mormon. One such passage came to mind when I attended a prayer breakfast at the White House in Washington, D.C., hosted by President Bill Clinton. During an informal reception that preceded the breakfast, I was chatting with a distinguished and scholarly Jewish rabbi from New York. Our conversation was interrupted by another rabbi who asked his colleague from New York if he could recall the scriptural reference to the stick of Judah and the stick of Joseph that would come together one day. My friend paused for a moment, stroked his chin pensively, and then replied, "I think you will find that in the book of Ezekiel."

With that, I could not restrain myself. "You might look in the thirty-seventh chapter of Ezekiel," I interjected. "There you will find the scriptures that you seek."

My rabbi friend expressed surprise: "How did *you* know that?"

"This doctrine," I concluded, "is very important in our theology."

Indeed it is. You know it, and I know it.

"Moreover, thou son of man, take thee one stick, and write upon it, For Judah, and for the children of Israel his companions: then take another stick, and write upon it, For Joseph, the stick of Ephraim, and for all the house of Israel his companions: And join them one to another into one stick; and they shall become one in thine hand" (Ezekiel 37:16–17).

Saints of modern Israel in 160 nations across the world are blessed to hold the Bible and the Book of Mormon as one in their hands. The worth of this privilege must never be underestimated.

Isaiah described the spirit of the Book of Mormon as "familiar" (Isaiah 29:4). It resonates with people who know the and Brigham Young organized a large group of men, women, and children for an orderly migration to the West.

We lament that leaders of both groups had to endure dissention from their close associates. On occasion, Moses encountered opposition from his beloved Aaron and Miriam (Numbers 12:2–11). Latter-day leaders also suffered contention among their trusted associates.[8] Nevertheless, that same unified pattern of government will come again when the Lord reigns as "King over all the earth" (Psalm 47:2; Zechariah 14:9) and governs from Zion and Jerusalem (Isaiah 2:1–4).

The journey from Egypt to Mt. Sinai took about three months (Exodus 12:2, 3, 6, 18; 13:4; 19:1). The journey from Winter Quarters to the valley of the Great Salt Lake also took about three months.[9]

The destination for each group was described by the Lord as a land "flowing with milk and honey."[10] The pioneers turned their wilderness into a fruitful field (Isaiah 32:15–16) and made the desert blossom as a rose (Isaiah 35:1)—precisely as prophesied by Isaiah centuries before.

Miracles Shared

Both groups shared many miracles that are memorialized annually. The celebration of Passover relates to the deliverance and exodus of the ancient Israelites. And each July, we honor and repeat legendary stories of our pioneers. Both groups traversed deserts, mountains, and valleys of untamed wilderness. Ancient Israelites left Egypt via the parted waters of the Red Sea "as by dry land" (Hebrews 11:29). The pioneers left the United States, crossing the wide waters of the Mississippi river—frozen to become a highway of ice.[11]

The book of Exodus reports that quail were miraculously provided to feed the hungry people of ancient Israel (Exodus 16:13; Numbers 11:32; Psalm 105:40). The pioneers had an equivalent experience. After the last of them had been driven out of Nauvoo, many were sick and some had died. Their provisions were meager. On the river bank above Montrose, Iowa, on October 9, 1846, many quail miraculously flew into camp. The quail were cooked and fed to 640 destitute people.[12] It was also miraculous that a permanent settlement survived in the valley of the Great Salt Lake. Seagulls that saved the crops were part of that miracle.

God preserved ancient Israel from plagues sent upon Egypt (Exodus 15:26). Similarly, God preserved the Saints from the plague of the U.S. Civil War that caused more American deaths than any other war.

Spiritual Strengths Shared

For both groups, their travail forged great spiritual strength among their people. They both endured trials of their faith during which the weak were winnowed away and the strong were empowered to endure to the end (Ether 12:6; D&C 101:4–5; 105:19). They had to leave their homes and earthly possessions and learn to rely wholly upon God. Protection was provided for ancient Israel by the Lord, who "went before them by day in a pillar of a cloud, to lead them the way; and by night in a pillar of fire" (Exodus 13:21; see also v. 22; Deuteronomy 1:33; Numbers 14:14; Nehemiah 9:19). The same has been said of divine watch care afforded to the pioneers.[13]

Scriptures given to both societies speak of the strength of the Lord's hand in their deliverance. To those of ancient Israel,

Moses said, "Remember this day, in which ye came out fr
Egypt, out of the house of bondage; for by strength of hand
Lord brought you out from this place" (Exodus 13:3).

To the Latter-day Saints, a comparable scripture was
vealed: "For I, the Lord, have put forth my hand to exert
powers of heaven; ye cannot see it now, yet a little while and
shall see it, and know that I am" (D&C 84:119).

The children of Israel had a portable tabernacle wher
they made covenants and performed ordinances to strengt
them on their journey.[14] Many Latter-day Saints were endo
in the Nauvoo Temple, which strengthened them spiritually
fore their arduous trek westward. The Israelites gratefully c
brated their exodus from Egypt. The Latter-day Sa
culminated their exodus with the establishment of world he
quarters of the restored Church in the tops of the mounta
All celebrants acclaimed their deliverance by God (Jerem
23:7).

Timeless Gospel Principles

Scriptures available to ancient and modern Israel incl
timeless principles of the gospel. We are familiar with
prophecy of Isaiah:

"Thou shalt be brought down, and shalt speak out of
ground, and thy speech shall be low out of the dust, and
voice shall be, as of one that hath a familiar spirit, out of
ground, and thy speech shall whisper out of the dust" (Is
29:4).

Could any words have been more descriptive of the B
of Mormon, coming as it did "out of the ground" to "whi
out of the dust" to people of our day?

Old Testament, especially those who are conversant with its Hebrew language. The Book of Mormon is rich with Hebraisms—traditions, symbolisms, idioms, and literary forms. It is familiar because more than 80 percent of its pages came from Old Testament times.[15]

Timeless truths and principles of the gospel were and are important to people of ancient and modern Israel. The Sabbath day, for example, was honored for different reasons through the generations. From the time of Adam to Moses, the Sabbath was observed as a day of rest from the labor of Creation (Exodus 20:8–11; 31:17). From the time of Moses to the Resurrection of the Lord, the Sabbath commemorated the liberation of the Israelites from their bondage in Egypt (Deuteronomy 5:12–15; Isaiah 58:13; Ezekiel 20:20; 44:24; Mosiah 13:19). In latter days, Saints keep the Sabbath day holy in memory of the Atonement of Jesus Christ (Acts 20:7; 1 Corinthians 16:2; Revelation 1:10; D&C 59:9–19).

The restoration of the priesthood rejuvenated the principle of tithing, linking to the Old Testament teachings of Genesis and Malachi (Genesis 14:20; Malachi 3:8–18). Saints of modern Israel know how to calculate their own tithing from this simple instruction:

"Those who have thus been tithed shall pay one-tenth of all their interest annually; and this shall be a standing law unto them forever, for my holy priesthood, saith the Lord" (D&C 119:4).

In contrast, have you ever amused yourself with the thought on or about April 15 each year that the filing of income tax returns is a bit more complicated? I'll confess that I have.

Turning our attention again to the timeless truths of the gospel, none are more vital than those associated with temple worship. They comprise another connection between ancient and modern Israel.

"Whenever the Lord has had a people on the earth who will obey his word, they have been commanded to build temples in which the ordinances of the gospel and other spiritual manifestations that pertain to exaltation and eternal life may be administered."[16]

The best known temple of ancient Israel was Solomon's temple. Its baptismal font (2 Chronicles 4:15) and dedicatory prayer (2 Chronicles 6:12–42) provided patterns that are employed for temples today (D&C 109:1–80). Old Testament scriptures refer to special clothing (Exodus 28:4; 29:5; Leviticus 8:7; 1 Samuel 18:4) and ordinances (Exodus 19:10, 14; Ezekiel 16:9; 2 Samuel 12:20) associated with temples (D&C 124:37–40). How thankful we are that the Lord chose to restore the highest blessings of the priesthood to His faithful sons and daughters. He said:

"For I deign to reveal unto my church things which have been kept hid from before the foundation of the world, things that pertain to the dispensation of the fulness of times" (D&C 124:41).

Revealed truth that we know as the Word of Wisdom came to the Prophet Joseph Smith in 1833. Every Latter-day Saint is familiar with it as one of the enduring hallmarks of our faith. The final verse of that revelation forges another link back to ancient Israel:

"And I, the Lord, give unto them a promise, that the destroying angel shall pass by them, as the children of Israel, and not slay them" (D&C 89:21).

This reference to the Passover shows that the Lord wanted obedient Saints of modern Israel to receive physical and spiritual protection just as He had provided for His faithful followers centuries before.

The Covenant, the Scattering, and the Gathering

Other divine teachings revered by both societies include doctrines of the Abrahamic covenant and of the scattering and gathering of Israel. About four thousand years ago, Abraham received a promise from the Lord that blessings would be offered to all of his mortal posterity (D&C 132:29–50; Abraham 2:6–11). Included were promises that the Son of God would come through Abraham's lineage, that certain lands would be inherited by his posterity, that nations and kindreds of the earth would be blessed through his seed, and more. Affirmation and reaffirmation of this covenant are evident in many scriptures of the Old Testament (Genesis 26:1–4, 24; 28; 35:9–13; 48:3–4).

While certain aspects of this covenant have already been fulfilled, many have not. The Book of Mormon teaches that we of modern Israel are among the covenant people of the Lord (1 Nephi 14:14; 15:14; 2 Nephi 30:2; Mosiah 24:13; 3 Nephi 29:3; Mormon 8:15). And most remarkably, it teaches that the Abrahamic covenant will be fulfilled only in the latter days! (1 Nephi 15:12–18).

Doctrines relating to the scattering and gathering of the house of Israel were among the earliest lessons taught in the Book of Mormon:

"After the house of Israel should be scattered they should be gathered together again; . . . the natural branches of the olive-tree, or the remnants of the house of Israel should be grafted in, or come to the knowledge of the true Messiah, their Lord and their Redeemer" (1 Nephi 10:14).

Saints of modern Israel know that Peter, James, and John were sent by the Lord with "the keys of [His] kingdom, and a dispensation of the gospel for the last times; and for the fulness of times," in which He would "gather together in one all things, both which are in heaven, and which are on earth" (D&C 27:13).[17]

The travels and travails of our pioneers were of eternal consequence. Their mission was not limited to an international immigration or a transcontinental migration with wagons and handcarts. They were to lay the foundation of an endless work that would "fill the world."[18] They were essential to Jeremiah's prophecy:

"Hear the word of the Lord, O ye nations, and declare it in the isles afar off and say, He that scattered Israel will gather him, and keep him, as a shepherd doth his flock" (Jeremiah 31:10).

The pioneer Saints got the message. Missionaries were soon sent to "the isles afar off" to commence the latter-day work of the Lord. As a result, the Church was established in the British Isles and in the islands of French Polynesia years before the pioneers entered the valley of the Great Salt Lake. It was my privilege to participate in sesquicentennial celebrations in the British Isles in 1987, in French Polynesia in 1994, and in Utah in 1997.

The lineage of Joseph—through Ephraim and Manasseh—is the seed appointed to lead in the gathering of Israel.[19] The pioneers knew—through their patriarchal blessings and from the Old Testament, amplified by scriptures and revelations of the Restoration—that the long-awaited gathering of Israel was to commence with them. This ball was in their court!

Summary

Early converts to The Church of Jesus Christ of Latter-day Saints were pioneers of modern Israel. Regardless of the time or place in which Saints may live, all faithful members of the Church will receive their just reward. "All things are theirs, whether life or death, or things present, or things to come, all are theirs and they are Christ's, and Christ is God's" (D&C 76:59).

Ancient and modern Israel subscribe to an ageless message of the Old Testament:

"Know therefore that the Lord thy God . . . keepeth covenant and mercy with them that love him and keep his commandments to a thousand generations" (Deuteronomy 7:9; see also Deuteronomy 11:1, 27; 19:9; 30:16; Joshua 22:5; 1 John 5:2–3; Mosiah 2:4).[20]

Upon our shoulders lies the responsibility to keep the faith through our own generation. This ball is in our court! We of modern Israel are destined to be "a kingdom of priests, and an holy nation" (Exodus 19:6). We know that we are children of the covenant (Acts 3:25; 3 Nephi 20:25–26). We are remnants of seed now to be gathered and gleaned into God's eternal garners (Alma 26:5).

Young adults are literally the hope of modern Israel. They are part of Zion's army. They are children of the promised day. I am grateful to be associated with them in the work of the Lord.

As Saints of modern Israel, we speak with one voice. We love our Heavenly Father. We love the Lord Jesus Christ, the Son of the living God. We are His people. We have taken His holy name upon us. We know the Book of Mormon to be the word of God and hold it as one with the Holy Bible. We proclaim Joseph Smith as the great prophet of the Restoration. And we sustain God's living prophets.

N<small>OTES</small>

From a Church Educational System fireside address, September 1997.

1. For more about these interrelationships, see JST, Genesis 50:26–38.
2. See J. Reuben Clark Jr., *On the Way to Immortality and Eternal Life* (Salt Lake City: Deseret Book, 1949), 153; Ezra Taft Benson, in Conference Report, April 1956, 58.
3. See Joseph Smith, *History of the Church of Jesus Christ of Latter-day Saints,* ed. B. H. Roberts, 2nd ed. rev., 7 vols. (Salt Lake City: The Church of Jesus Christ of Latter-day Saints, 1932–51) 2:6, 185.
4. See *History of the Church,* 2:529.
5. See *History of the Church,* 3:252, 261.
6. See *Teachings of the Prophet Joseph Smith,* sel. Joseph Fielding Smith (Salt Lake City: Deseret Book, 1976), 252.
7. President Spencer W. Kimball wrote of Brigham Young's role in that exodus: "Since Adam there have been many exoduses and promised lands: Abraham, Jared, Moses, Lehi, and others led groups. How easy it is to accept those distant in time as directed by the Lord, yet the ones near at hand as human calculations and decisions. Let us consider for a moment the great trek of the Mormon refugees from Illinois to Salt Lake Valley. Few, if any, great movements equal it. We frequently hear that Brigham Young led the people to make new tracks in a desert and to climb over mountains seldom scaled and to ford and wade unbridged rivers and to traverse a hostile Indian country; and while Brigham Young was the instrument of the Lord, it was not he but the Lord of heaven who led modern Israel across the plains to their promised land" (*Faith Precedes the Miracle* [Salt Lake City: Deseret Book, 1972], 28).
8. For examples, see *History of the Church,* 1:104–5 (pertaining to Oliver Cowdery) and *History of the Church,* 1:226 (pertaining to William E. McLellin).
9. One hundred and eleven days.
10. For the people of ancient Israel, see Exodus 3:8, 17; 13:5; 33:3; Leviticus 20:24; Numbers 13:27; 14:8; 16:13–14; Deuteronomy 6:3; 11:9; 26:9, 15; 27:3; 31:20; Joshua 5:6; Jeremiah 11:5; 32:22; Ezekiel 20:6, 15; JST, Exodus 33:1. For the pioneers, see D&C 38:18–19.
11. See Orson Pratt, in *Journal of Discourses,* 26 vols. (London: Latter-day Saints' Book Depot, 1854–86), 21:275–77.

12. See Stanley B. Kimball, "Nauvoo West: The Mormons on the Iowa Shore," *BYU Studies* 18, no. 2 (Winter 1978): 142. *Catching Quails,* an oil painting on canvas by C. C. A. Christensen, is in the Museum of Fine Arts at Brigham Young University.

13. See *History of the Church,* 3:34; Thomas S. Monson, in Conference Report, April 1967, 56.

14. Ordinances and covenants of ancient Israel cited in 1 Corinthians 10:1–3; for modern Israel, see D&C 84:26–27. Originally, before the people had lost the higher law, the tabernacle was intended to be a movable temple (D&C 84:25; 124:38).

15. Personal communication from Elder Jeffrey R. Holland.

16. Bible Dictionary, "Temple," 781.

17. Compare this with Paul's prophecy of the Restoration in Ephesians 1:10.

18. Statement of Joseph Smith as reported by Wilford Woodruff, in *The Discourses of Wilford Woodruff,* sel. and ed. G. Homer Durham (Salt Lake City: Bookcraft, 1946), 38–39.

19. See Erastus Snow, in *Journal of Discourses,* 23:182.

20. Other Old Testament scriptures refer to rewards for those obedient to God's commandments through a "thousand generations" (1 Chronicles 16:15; Psalm 105:8).

11

Christt the Savior Is Born

Through all of our various Christmas traditions, I hope that we are focused first upon the Lord Jesus Christ. Wise men still adore Him. We commemorate His humble birth at this time of year, even though we know it did not occur in December but rather in April. Scriptures declare that His mother, Mary, was espoused to Joseph. They had participated in the first of two components of a Jewish marriage ceremony. Their espousal might be likened to an engagement in our culture, which is followed later by the second component of a marriage ceremony.

Luke's account records the appearance of the Angel Gabriel to Mary when she learned of her favored future:

"Hail, thou that art highly favoured, . . . blessed art thou among women. . . . And the angel said unto her, Fear not, Mary: for thou hast found favour with God. And, behold, thou shalt conceive in thy womb, and bring forth a son, and shalt call his name Jesus. He shall be great, and shall be called the Son of the Highest" (Luke 1:28, 30–32).[1]

God is the Highest. Jesus was to be the Son of the Highest.

"Then said Mary unto the angel, How shall this be, seeing I know not a man?" (Luke 1:34).

She knew of her virginal status.

"And the angel answered and said unto her, The Holy Ghost shall come upon thee, and the power of the Highest shall overshadow thee: therefore also that holy thing which shall be born of thee shall be called the Son of God" (Luke 1:35).

Before Joseph and Mary came together, she was expecting that holy child. Joseph desired to protect her privacy (Matthew 1:18–19), hoping to spare Mary the punishment given to a woman pregnant without a completed marriage. While he pondered these things, the Angel Gabriel appeared to Joseph, saying:

"Joseph, thou son of David, fear not to take unto thee Mary thy wife: for that which is conceived in her is of the Holy Ghost. And she shall bring forth a son, and thou shalt call his name Jesus: for he shall save his people from their sins" (Matthew 1:20–21).

Mary and Joseph did not need to be taught the deep significance of the name *Jesus*. The Hebrew root from which it was derived, *Jehoshua*, means "Jehovah is salvation." So the mission of Jehovah, soon to be named Jesus, was salvation, and His supreme destiny was to become the Savior of the world.

Let's turn to the Book of Mormon for the dialogue that Nephi had with an angel:

The angel asked, "Knowest thou the condescension of God?" (1 Nephi 11:16).

Nephi replied, "I know that he loveth his children;

nevertheless, I do not know the meaning of all things. And he said unto me: Behold, the virgin whom thou seest is the mother of the Son of God, after the manner of the flesh. . . . I beheld that she was carried away in the Spirit; and after she had been carried away in the Spirit for the space of a time the angel spake unto me, saying: Look! And I looked and beheld the virgin again, bearing a child in her arms. And the angel said unto me: Behold the Lamb of God, yea, even the Son of the Eternal Father!" (1 Nephi 11:17–21).

Now let's turn to the second chapter of Luke—the fond and familiar story we read at Christmas time:

"And it came to pass in those days, that there went out a decree from Caesar Augustus, that all the world should be taxed" (Luke 2:1).

This was really a capitation tax, a census, an enrollment—a registration of the citizenry of the empire of Rome. Herod had made a decision that people should be counted in the land of their ancestors. Mary and Joseph, then living in Nazareth, had to travel southward to the city of David, a distance of approximately seventy miles. Perhaps they traveled even farther if they went around the hostile intermediate province of Samaria. Almost certainly they traveled with relatives who likewise were summoned to the land of their ancestry. This difficult journey was no doubt made with their animals, such as dogs and donkeys. They likely camped out several nights because three to four days would have been required for the journey.

"And she brought forth her firstborn son, and wrapped him in swaddling clothes, and laid him in a manger; because there was no room for them in the inn" (Luke 2:7).

Let's pause to ponder this verse. We need to be aware of the culture of that time and region, and we need to learn one word from the original Greek text. In the Greek New Testament, the root from which "inn" was translated is *kataluma*. We don't have an equivalent word in the English language. The Greek prefix *kata* (or *cata)* means "a bringing down." We see it in English words such as *cata*bolism, *cata*strophe, and *cata*clysm. When the prefix *kata* was joined with the suffix *luma,* it meant literally "a breaking down of a journey." A *kataluma* was a guest chamber in a lodging place.

In those days, an inn was not like a Holiday Inn or a "Bethlehem Marriott." A lodging place in that part of Asia had to provide accommodations for traveling caravans, including the people and their animals. Caravans stayed at what was then known (and is still known) as a *caravansary,* or a *khan.* Each is defined as a rest house in some Asian countries.

Such a facility is typically rectangular in shape. It is composed of a central courtyard for the animals, surrounded by walled cubicles where the people rest. These quarters, with open doorways so that owners could watch over their animals, allowed guests to be elevated slightly above their animals.

The Joseph Smith Translation of Luke 2:7 indicates that there was no room for them in the "inns," suggesting that all of the *katalumas,* or cubicles of the caravansary, were occupied. In the Greek New Testament, the word *kataluma* appears in only two other passages (Mark 14:14; Luke 22:11), translated in each instance not as "inn" but as "guest chamber," which fits the concept discussed above.

As a youngster, whenever I heard the words "no room in the inn," I assumed that "no vacancy" signs were posted at local motels or that the innkeepers were inhospitable or even hostile. Such an assumption is probably way off the mark. People of that part of the world were no doubt then, as they are now, most hospitable. Particularly this would have been true at a season when the normal population of Jerusalem and neighboring Bethlehem would be swollen with large numbers of relatives.

At a caravansary, animals were secured for the night in the center courtyard. In that courtyard, there would have been donkeys and dogs, sheep, possibly camels and oxen, along with all of the animals' discharges and odors. Because the guest chambers surrounding the courtyard were filled, Joseph possibly made the decision to care for Mary's delivery in the center courtyard of a caravansary—among the animals. There, in that lowly circumstance, the Lamb of God was born.

Why was reference made twice in Luke 2 to His being wrapped in swaddling clothes? (Luke 2:7, 12). What is the meaning of those five words: "wrapped him in swaddling clothes"? I sense a significance beyond the use of an ordinary diaper and receiving blanket. Instead of those five words in the English text, only one word is needed in the Greek New Testament. That word is *sparganoo,* which means to envelop a newborn child with special cloth, strips of which were passed from side to side.[2] The cloth would probably bear unique family identification. That procedure was especially applicable to the birth of a firstborn son.

You remember the announcement of an angel at the birth of Jesus:

"This shall be a sign unto you; Ye shall find the babe wrapped in swaddling clothes, lying in a manger" (Luke 2:12). His wrappings surely would have been distinctive.

I think that such a concept of a cloth with family markings might also have been relevant when Joseph, son of Israel, became the birthright son and received the unique cloth coat of many colors—a fabric symbolic of the birthright.

What about the manger? Those who speak French will recognize the word to be the same as the French word *manger,* meaning "to eat." A manger is a trough or an open box in a stable designed to hold feed or fodder for animals to eat. Elevated from the floor of the contaminated courtyard, a manger was probably the cleanest site available. Such a feeding trough became the cradle for our Lord!

Now two millennia later, though we don't know all the details pertaining to His birth, we certainly understand the unique parentage of this Babe of Bethlehem. Several scriptures ask the question: "Who shall declare His generation?" (Isaiah 53:8; Acts 8:33; Mosiah 14:8; 15:10). We declare solemnly and with conviction: Jesus was born of an immortal Father and a mortal mother. From His immortal Father, Jesus inherited the power to live forever. From His mortal mother, He inherited the fate of physical death.

He declared this reality regarding His own life: "No man taketh it from me," He said, "but I lay it down of myself. I have power to lay it down, and I have power to take it again. This commandment have I received of my Father" (John 10:18).

Those unique attributes were essential for His mission to atone for the sins of all mankind. Thus Jesus the Christ was born to die (3 Nephi 27:13–14). He died that we might live. He was born that all humankind could live beyond the grave (3 Nephi 27:14–15). His Atonement was wrought in Gethsemane, where He sweat great drops of blood, and on Golgotha (or Calvary), where His body was lifted up upon a cross—over the place of the skull, which signified death. This infinite Atonement would release man from the infinitude of death (2 Nephi 9:7). His Atonement made the resurrection a reality and the gift of eternal life a possibility for all who would obey His teachings. His Atonement became the central act of all human history.

Our recollections of Christmas are enriched by these

realities. Each one of us with a testimony of the Lord has the privilege in faith to know of His divine parentage and to testify that Jesus is the Son of the living God.

True testimony includes the fact that the Father and the Son appeared to the Prophet Joseph Smith, whose birth we commemorate on December 23. That testimony includes the fact that The Church of Jesus Christ of Latter-day Saints is true and is led by the living Lord via prophecy and revelation through authorized administrators who receive and respond to direction from Him.

With this background in mind, I share comforting counsel. It comes from section 68 of the Doctrine and Covenants, where we read this commandment from our Master: "Be of good cheer, and do not fear, for I the Lord am with you, and will stand by you; and ye shall bear record of me, even Jesus Christ, that I am the Son of the living God, that I was, that I am and that I am to come" (D&C 68:6).

Lovingly, we cling to that promise. Difficult days are ahead for all mankind. Sin is on the increase. We live in a time of wars and rumors of wars. The Church and its members will come under attack and endure persecution (2 Timothy 3:1–13; D&C 112:24).

Jesus descended below all things in order to rise above all things. He expects us to follow His example. Yoked with Him, we can rise above all challenges, no matter how difficult they may be (Matthew 11:29–30). Peter offered this counsel:

"If any man suffer as a Christian, let him not be ashamed; but let him glorify God on this behalf" (1 Peter 4:16).

The time is coming when those who do *not* obey the Lord will be separated from those who *do*. Our safest insurance is to continue to be worthy of admission to His holy house. How blessed we are to have temples. The greatest gift you could give to the Lord any time of year is to keep yourself unspotted from the world, worthy to attend His holy house. His gift to you will be the peace and security of knowing that you are worthy to meet Him, whenever that time comes.

I plead with you to rise above the tasks of the day and the hurdles ahead. You can do more than the deeds scheduled in your daily planners. You can take the name of the Lord upon you and become more like Him. You can rise to your great potential. You can prepare for the future with greater spiritual capacity.

Remember that the fulness of Christ's ministry lies in the future. The prophecies of His Second Coming have yet to be fulfilled. At Christmas, of course, we focus upon His birth. But He will come again. At His First Coming, Jesus came almost in secret. Only a few mortals knew of His birth. At His Second Coming, the whole of humankind will know of His return. Then He will come, not as "a man traveling on the earth" (D&C 49:22), but His glory "shall be revealed, and all flesh shall see it together" (Isaiah 40:5; see also D&C 101:23).

As a special witness of His holy name, I testify that Jesus is the divine Son of the living God. He will love you, lift you, and manifest Himself unto you if you will love Him and keep His commandments (John 14:21).

NOTES

From a Brigham Young University devotional address, December 2002.

1. Note the capital S and H.
2. See word number 4,683 in James Strong, *Abingdon's Strong's Exhaustive Concordance of the Bible,* Greek Dictionary of the New Testament (Nashville: Abingdon Press, 1978), 66.

Personal
Growth

12

Personal Preparation for Temple Blessings

U nder President Gordon B. Hinckley's inspired direction, temples are now more accessible than ever. Inscribed on each temple are the words "Holiness to the Lord" (Exodus 28:36; 39:30; Psalm 93:5).[1] That statement designates both the temple and its purposes as holy. Those who enter the temple are also to bear the attribute of holiness (Exodus 19:5–6; Leviticus 19:1–2; Psalm 24:3–5; 1 Thessalonians 4:7; Moroni 10:32–33; D&C 20:69; 110:6–9).[2] It may be easier to ascribe holiness to a building than to a people. We can acquire holiness only by enduring and persistent personal effort. Through the ages, servants of the Lord have warned against unholiness. Jacob, brother of Nephi, wrote, "I would speak unto you of holiness; but as ye are not holy, and ye look upon me as a teacher, [I] must . . . teach you the consequences of sin" (2 Nephi 9:48).

I feel that same sense of responsibility to teach. As temples are prepared for our members, our members need to prepare for the temple.

The Temple

The temple is the house of the Lord. The basis for every temple ordinance and covenant—the heart of the plan of salvation—is the Atonement of Jesus Christ. Every activity, every lesson, all we do in the Church points to the Lord and His holy house. Our efforts to proclaim the gospel, perfect the Saints, and redeem the dead all lead to the temple. Each holy temple stands as a symbol of our membership in the Church,[3] as a sign of our faith in life after death, and as a sacred step toward eternal glory for our families and us.

President Hinckley said that "these unique and wonderful buildings, and the ordinances administered therein, represent the ultimate in our worship. These ordinances become the most profound expressions of our theology."[4]

To enter the temple is a tremendous blessing. But first we must be worthy. We should not be rushed. We cannot cut corners of preparation and risk the breaking of covenants we were not prepared to make. That would be worse than not making them at all.

The Endowment

In the temple we receive an endowment, which is, literally speaking, a gift. In receiving this gift, we should understand its significance and the importance of keeping sacred covenants.

Each temple ordinance "is not just a ritual to go through, it is an act of solemn promising."[5]

The temple endowment was given by revelation. Thus, it is best understood by revelation, prayerfully sought with a sincere heart (Moroni 10:4–5). President Brigham Young said, "Your endowment is, to receive all those ordinances in the house of the Lord, which are necessary for you, after you have departed this life, to enable you to walk back to the presence of the Father, . . . and gain your eternal exaltation."[6]

Sealing Authority

In preparing to receive the endowment and other ordinances of the temple, we should understand the sealing authority of the priesthood. Jesus referred to this authority long ago when He taught His Apostles: "Whatsoever thou shalt bind on earth shall be bound in heaven" (Matthew 16:19). That same authority has been restored in these latter days. Just as priesthood is eternal—without beginning or end—so is the effect of priesthood ordinances that bind families together forever.

Temple ordinances, covenants, endowments, and sealings enable individuals to be reconciled with the Lord, and they enable families to be sealed beyond the veil of death. Obedience to temple covenants qualifies us for eternal life, the greatest gift of God to man (D&C 14:7). Eternal life is more than immortality. Eternal life is exaltation in the highest heaven—the kind of life that God lives.

Temple Recommend

Preparation also includes qualification for a temple recommend. Our Redeemer requires that His temples be protected from desecration. No unclean thing may enter His hallowed house (D&C 109:20; see also Isaiah 52:11; Alma 11:37; 3 Nephi 27:19). Yet anyone is welcome who prepares well. Each person applying for a recommend will be interviewed by a judge in Israel—the bishop—and by a stake president (or the branch president and mission president). They hold keys of priesthood authority and the responsibility to help us know when our preparation and timing are appropriate to enter the temple. Their interviews will assess several vital issues. They will ask if we obey the law of tithing, if we keep the Word of Wisdom, and if we sustain the authorities of the Church. They will ask if we are honest, if we are morally clean, and if we honor the power of procreation as a sacred trust from our Creator.

Why are these issues so crucial? Because they are spiritual separators. They help to determine if we truly live as children of the covenant (3 Nephi 20:26),[7] able to resist temptation from servants of sin (Romans 6:17, 20; D&C 121:17). These interviews help to discern if we are willing to live in accord with the will of the true and living God or if our hearts are still set "upon riches and . . . vain things of the world" (Alma 7:6).

Such requirements are not difficult to understand. Because the temple is the house of the Lord, standards for admission are set by Him. One enters as His guest. To hold a temple recommend is a priceless privilege and a tangible sign of obedience to God and His prophets.[8]

Physical Preparation for the Temple

One prepares physically for the temple by dressing properly. It is not a place for casual attire. "We should dress in such a way that we might comfortably attend a sacrament meeting or a gathering that is proper and dignified."[9]

Within the temple, all are dressed in spotless white to remind us that God is to have a pure people.[10] Nationality, language, or position in the Church are of secondary significance. In that democracy of dress, all sit side by side and are considered equal in the eyes of our Maker.[11]

Brides and grooms enter the temple to be married for time and all eternity. There brides wear white dresses—long sleeved, modest in design and fabric, and free of elaborate ornamentation. Grooms also dress in white. And brethren who come to witness weddings do not wear tuxedos.

Wearing the temple garment has deep symbolic significance. It represents a continuing commitment.[12] Surely we would not ever knowingly want to discard from us an emblem of God's everlasting covenant. Just as the Savior exemplified the need to endure to the end, we wear the garment faithfully as part of the enduring armor of God (Ephesians 6:11–13; see also Alma 46:13, 21; D&C 27:15). Thus we demonstrate our faith in Him and in His eternal covenants with us.[13]

Spiritual Preparation for the Temple

In addition to physical preparation, we prepare spiritually. Because the ordinances and covenants of the temple are sacred, we are under solemn obligation not to speak outside the temple of that which occurs in the temple. There are, however, some principles we can discuss.

Each temple is a house of learning (D&C 88:119; 109:8). There we are taught in the Master's way.[14] His way differs from modes of others. His way is ancient and rich with symbolism. We can learn much by pondering the reality for which each symbol stands.[15] Teachings of the temple are beautifully simple and simply beautiful. They are understood by the humble, yet they can excite the intellect of the brightest minds.

Spiritual preparation is enhanced by study. I like to recommend that members going to the temple for the first time read short explanatory paragraphs in the Bible Dictionary, listed under seven topics:[16] "Anoint,"[17] "Atonement,"[18] "Christ,"[19] "Covenant,"[20] "Fall of Adam,"[21] "Sacrifices,"[22] and "Temple."[23] Doing so will provide a firm foundation.

One may also read in the Old Testament[24] and the books of Moses and Abraham in the Pearl of Great Price. Such a review of ancient scripture is even more enlightening *after* one is familiar with the temple endowment. Those books underscore the antiquity of temple work (D&C 124:40–41).

With each ordinance is a covenant—a promise. A covenant made with God is not restrictive but rather protective. Such a concept is not new. For example, if our water supply is not clean, we filter the water to screen out harmful ingredients. Divine covenants help us to filter out of our minds impurities that could harm us. When we choose to deny ourselves of all ungodliness (Moroni 10:32; JST, Matthew 16:26), we lose nothing of value and gain the glory of eternal life. Covenants do not hold us down; they elevate us beyond the limits of our own power and perspective.

Eternal Perspective

President Hinckley explained that lofty perspective: "There is a goal beyond the Resurrection," he said. "That is exaltation in our Father's kingdom. . . . It will begin with acceptance of him as our Eternal Father and of his son as our living Redeemer. It will involve participation in various ordinances, each one important and necessary. The first of these is baptism by immersion in water, without which, according to the Savior, a man cannot enter into the kingdom of God. There must follow the birth of the Spirit, the gift of the Holy Ghost. Then in succession through the years will come, for men, ordination to the priesthood, followed by the blessings of the temple for both men and women who are worthy to enter therein. These temple blessings include our washings and anointings that we may be clean before the Lord. They include the . . . endowment of obligations and blessings that motivate us to behavior compatible with the principles of the gospel. They include the sealing ordinances by which that which is bound on earth is bound in heaven, providing for the continuity of the family."[25]

I have learned that temple blessings are most meaningful when death takes a loved one away from the family circle. To know that the pain of separation is only temporary provides peace that passes ordinary understanding (Philippians 4:7). Death cannot sever families sealed in the temple. They understand death as a necessary part of God's great plan of happiness (Alma 42:8).

Such perspective helps us to maintain fidelity to covenants made. President Boyd K. Packer emphasized that "ordinances and covenants become our credentials for admission into [God's] presence. To worthily receive them is the quest of a lifetime; to keep them thereafter is the challenge of mortality."[26]

Ordinances of the temple relate to *personal* progress and to the redemption of departed *ancestors* as well. "For their salvation is necessary and essential to our salvation, . . . they without us cannot be made perfect—neither can we without our dead be made perfect" (D&C 128:15). Service in their behalf provides repeated opportunities for temple worship. And that service deserves commitment to a planned schedule. By doing for others what they cannot do for themselves, we emulate the pattern of the Savior, who wrought the Atonement to bless the lives of other people.

One day we will meet our Maker and stand before Him at the Judgment (2 Nephi 9:41). We will be judged according to our ordinances, covenants, deeds, and the desires of our hearts (D&C 137:9).

Meanwhile, in this world smitten with spiritual decay, can individuals prepared for temple blessings make a difference? Yes! Those Saints are "the covenant people of the Lord, . . . armed with righteousness and with the power of God in great glory" (1 Nephi 14:14). Their example can lift the lives of all humankind.

NOTES

From a talk given at general conference, March 2001.

1. Translated equivalents are used on temples throughout the world.
2. See also Bible Dictionary, "Holiness," 703–4.
3. See "Following the Master: Teachings of President Howard W. Hunter," *Ensign,* April 1995, 21–22; Howard W. Hunter, "The Great Symbol of Our Membership," *Ensign,* October 1994, 2.
4. Gordon B. Hinckley, "Of Missions, Temples, and Stewardship," *Ensign,* November 1995, 53.
5. Gordon B. Hinckley, *Teachings of Gordon B. Hinckley* (Salt Lake City: Deseret Book, 1997), 638.

6. *Discourses of Brigham Young,* sel. John A. Widtsoe (Salt Lake City: Deseret Book, 1941), 416.

7. See also Russell M. Nelson, "Children of the Covenant," *Ensign,* May 1995, 32.

8. President Hinckley said, "I urge our people everywhere, with all of the persuasiveness of which I am capable, to live worthy to hold a temple recommend, to secure one and regard it as a precious asset, and to make a greater effort to go to the house of the Lord and partake of the spirit and the blessings to be had therein" ("Of Missions, Temples, and Stewardship," 53).

9. Boyd K. Packer, *The Holy Temple* (Salt Lake City: Bookcraft, 1980), 73.

10. See Neal A. Maxwell, *Not My Will, but Thine* (Salt Lake City: Deseret Book, 1988), 135; see also D&C 100:16.

11. This reminds us that "God is no respecter of persons" (Acts 10:34; see also Moroni 8:12).

12. The Lord assured that even though "the mountains shall depart, and the hills be removed; . . . my kindness shall not depart from thee, neither shall the covenant of my people be removed" (JST, Isaiah 54:10).

13. In a letter dated October 10, 1988, the First Presidency wrote: "Practices frequently observed among the members of the Church suggest that some members do not fully understand the covenant they make in the temple to wear the garment in accordance with the spirit of the holy endowment.

"Church members who have been clothed with the garment in the temple have made a covenant to wear it throughout their lives. This has been interpreted to mean that it is worn as underclothing both day and night. . . . The promise of protection and blessings is conditioned upon worthiness and faithfulness in keeping the covenant.

"The fundamental principle ought to be to wear the garment and not to find occasions to remove it. Thus, members should not remove either all or part of the garment to work in the yard or to lounge around the home in swimwear or immodest clothing. Nor should they remove it to participate in recreational activities that can reasonably be done with the garment worn properly beneath regular clothing. When the garment must be removed, such as for swimming, it should be restored as soon as possible.

"The principles of modesty and keeping the body appropriately covered are implicit in the covenant and should govern the nature of all clothing worn. Endowed members of the Church wear the garment as a reminder of the sacred covenants they have made with the Lord and also as a protection against temptation and evil. How it is worn is an outward expression of an inward commitment to follow the Savior."

14. In fact, He *is* the way (John 14:6).

15. See John A. Widtsoe, "Temple Worship," *Utah Genealogical and Historical Magazine,* April 1921, 62.

16. Members of the Church who do not read English may find comparable terms in their language editions of the "Guide to the Scriptures."

17. Bible Dictionary, 609, paragraphs 1, 4.

18. Bible Dictionary, 617, paragraphs 1–2.

19. Bible Dictionary, 633, paragraphs 1–3.

20. Bible Dictionary, 651, paragraphs 1–2.

21. Bible Dictionary, 670, paragraphs 1–2.

22. Bible Dictionary, 765–66, paragraph 1.

23. Bible Dictionary, 780–81, paragraphs 1–3.

24. Chapters of special interest include Exodus 26–29, 39; Leviticus 8; 2 Samuel 12 (v. 20); 2 Chronicles 6–7; Isaiah 22; Ezekiel 16.

25. Gordon B. Hinckley, "Temples and Temple Work," *Ensign,* February 1982, 3.

26. Boyd K. Packer, "Covenants," *Ensign,* May 1987, 24.

13

Repentance and Conversion

While Elder David S. Baxter and I were driving to a stake conference some time ago, we stopped at a restaurant. Later, when returning to our car, we were approached by a woman who called out to us. We were startled by her appearance. Her grooming (or lack of it) was what I might politely call *extreme*. She asked if we were elders in the Church. We said yes. Almost unrestrained, she told the story of her tragic life, swamped in sin. Now, only twenty-eight years old, she was miserable. She felt worthless, with nothing to live for. As she spoke, the sweetness of her soul began to emerge. Pleading tearfully, she asked if there was any hope for her, any way up and out of her hopelessness.

"Yes," we responded, "there is hope. Hope is linked to repentance. You can change. You can 'come unto Christ, and be perfected in him'" (Moroni 10:32). We urged her not to procrastinate (see Alma 13:27; 34:33).[1] She sobbed humbly and thanked us sincerely.

As Elder Baxter and I continued our journey, we pondered that experience. We recalled the counsel given to a hopeless soul by Aaron, who said, "If thou wilt repent of all thy sins, and will bow down before God, and call on his name in faith, . . . then shalt thou receive the hope which thou desirest" (Alma 22:16).[2]

The Lord has commanded His servants to cry repentance unto all people (D&C 18:11–12, 14; 19:21; 34:5–6; 43:20; 133:16–17).[3] The Master has restored His gospel to bring joy to His children, and repentance is a crucial component of that gospel.[4]

The doctrine of repentance is as old as the gospel itself. Biblical teachings from the books of Genesis (Genesis 4:8) to Revelation (Revelation 2:16) teach repentance. Lessons from Jesus Christ during His mortal ministry include these warnings: "The kingdom of God is at hand: repent ye, and believe the gospel" (Mark 1:15; see also Matthew 4:17) and "Except ye repent, ye shall all likewise perish" (Luke 13:3).

References to repentance are even more frequent in the Book of Mormon. The word *repent* (to teach the doctrine of repentance) in any of its forms (*repent, repentance, repented, repenteth,* and so on) appears 72 times in the King James Version of the Bible and 68 times in the Joseph Smith Translation of the Bible. In the Book of Mormon, however, the word *repent* in any of its forms appears 360 times. To the people of ancient America, the Lord gave this commandment: "Again I say unto you, ye must repent, and be baptized in my name, and become as a little child, or ye can in nowise inherit the kingdom of God" (3 Nephi 11:38).[5]

With the Restoration of the gospel, our Savior has again stressed this doctrine. The word *repent* in any of its forms appears in 47 of the 138 sections of the Doctrine and Covenants! (D&C 1; 3; 5–6; 10–11; 13–16; 18–20; 29; 33–36; 39; 42–45; 49–50; 53–56; 58; 63–64; 66; 68; 75; 84; 90; 93; 98; 104; 107; 109; 117; 124; 133; 136; 138).

Repent from Sin

What does it mean to repent? We begin with a dictionary's definition that to repent is "to turn from sin . . . to feel sorrow [and] regret."[6] To repent from sin is not easy. But the prize is worth the price. Repentance needs to be done one step at a time. Humble prayer will facilitate each essential step. As prerequisites to forgiveness, there must first be recognition, remorse, and then confession (1 John 1:9; Mosiah 26:29; D&C 61:2; 64:7).

"By this ye may know if a man repenteth of his sins—behold, he will confess them and forsake them" (D&C 58:43).[7] Confession is to be made to the person who has been wronged. Confession should be sincere and not merely an admission of guilt after proof is evident. If many persons have been offended, confession should be made to all offended parties. Acts that may affect one's standing in the Church or the right to its privileges should be confessed promptly to the bishop, whom the Lord has called as a common judge in Israel (D&C 107:73–74).

The next step is restitution—to repair damage done—if possible. Then come steps to resolve to do better and refrain from relapse—to repent "with full purpose of heart" (2 Nephi 31:13; Jacob 6:5; Mosiah 7:33; 3 Nephi 10:6; 12:24; 18:32). Thanks to the ransom paid by the Atonement of Jesus Christ, full forgiveness is given to the sinner who repents and remains free from sin (Mosiah 4:2–3). To the repentant soul, Isaiah said, "Though your sins be as scarlet, they shall be as white as snow; though they be red like crimson, they shall be as wool" (Isaiah 1:18).

The Lord's imperative emphasis on repentance is evident as we read from section 19 of the Doctrine and Covenants: "I command you to repent—repent, lest I smite you by the rod of my mouth, and by my wrath, and by my anger, and your sufferings be sore—how sore you know not, how exquisite you know not, yea, how hard to bear you know not. For behold, I, God, have suffered these things for all, that they might not suffer if they would repent; but if they would not repent they must suffer even as I" (vv. 15–17).

While the Lord insists on our repentance, most people don't feel such a compelling need.[8] They include themselves among those who try to be good. They have no evil intent.[9] Yet the Lord is clear in His message that *all* need to repent—not only from sins of *commission* but from sins of *omission* as well. Such is the case in His warning to parents: "Inasmuch as parents have children in Zion . . . that teach them *not* to understand the doctrine of repentance, faith in Christ the Son of the living God, and of baptism and the gift of the Holy Ghost . . . , the sin be upon the heads of the parents" (D&C 68:25; emphasis added).

Broader Meaning of the Word *Repent*

The doctrine of repentance is much broader than a dictionary's definition. When Jesus said "repent," His disciples recorded the command in the Greek language with the verb *metanoeo*.[10] This powerful word has great significance. In this word the prefix *meta* means "change."[11] The suffix relates to four important Greek terms: *nous,* meaning "the mind"[12]; *gnosis,* meaning "knowledge"[13]; *pneuma,* meaning "spirit"[14]; and *pnoe,* meaning "breath."[15]

Thus, when Jesus said "repent," He asked us to change—to change our mind, knowledge, spirit, and even our breath. A prophet explained that such a change in one's breath is to breathe with grateful acknowledgment of Him who grants each breath. King Benjamin said, "If ye should serve him who has created you . . . and is preserving you from day to day, by lending you breath . . . from one moment to another—I say, if ye should serve him with all your whole souls yet ye would be unprofitable servants" (Mosiah 2:21).

Yes, the Lord has commanded us to repent, to change our ways, to come unto Him, and be more like Him (3 Nephi 27:21, 27). This requires a total change. Alma so taught his son: "Learn wisdom in thy youth; yea, learn in thy youth to keep the commandments of God. . . . Let all thy thoughts be directed unto the Lord; yea, let the affections of thy heart be placed upon the Lord forever" (Alma 37:35–36).

To repent fully is to convert completely to the Lord Jesus Christ and His holy work. Alma taught that concept when he posed these questions: "I ask of you, my brethren of the church, have ye spiritually been born of God? Have ye received his image in your countenances? Have ye experienced this mighty change in your hearts?" (Alma 5:14). That change comes when we are "born again" (John 3:3, 7; Mosiah 27:25; Alma 5:49; 7:14; Moses 6:59), converted and focused upon our journey to the kingdom of God.

Fruits of Repentance

The fruits of repentance are sweet. Repentant converts find that the truths of the restored gospel govern their thoughts and deeds, shape their habits, and forge their character. They are more resilient and able to deny themselves of all ungodliness (Moroni 10:32). Moreover, uncontrolled appetite (Galatians 6:7–8), addiction to pornography or harmful drugs (Judges 13:7; Luke 1:15; D&C 89:5, 7–9), unbridled passion (Matthew 5:27–28; Alma 38:12; 3 Nephi 12:27–28; D&C 42:23), carnal desire (Romans 8:5–6), and unrighteous pride (Alma 38:11; D&C 121:37) are diminished with complete conversion to the Lord and a determination to serve Him and to emulate His example (John 13:15; 1 Timothy 4:12; 1 Peter 2:21; 2 Nephi 31:16; 3 Nephi 18:16; Mormon 7:10). Virtue garnishes their thoughts, and their self-confidence grows (D&C 121:45). Tithing is seen as a joyful and protective blessing, not as a duty or a sacrifice (D&C 85:3). Truth becomes more attractive, and things praiseworthy become more engaging (Philippians 4:8; Articles of Faith 1:13).

Repentance is the Lord's regimen for spiritual growth. King Benjamin explained that "the natural man is an enemy to God, and has been from the fall of Adam, and will be, forever and ever, unless he yields to the enticings of the Holy Spirit, and putteth off the natural man and becometh a saint through the atonement of Christ the Lord, and becometh as a child, submissive, meek, humble, patient, full of love, willing to submit to all things which the Lord seeth fit to inflict upon him, even as a child doth submit to his father" (Mosiah 3:19). That means conversion! Repentance is conversion! A repentant soul is a converted soul, and a converted soul is a repentant soul.

Repentance for Those Who Are Dead

Each living person can repent. But what about those who have died? They also have opportunities to repent. Scripture declares that "the faithful elders of this dispensation, when they depart from mortal life, continue their labors in the preaching of the gospel of repentance . . . among those who are . . . under the bondage of sin in the great world of the spirits of the dead. The dead who repent will be redeemed, through obedience to the ordinances of the house of God, and after they have paid the penalty of their transgressions, and are washed clean, [they] shall receive a reward according to their works" (D&C 138:57–59; see also vv. 30–34).

The Prophet Joseph Smith further revealed that "the earth will be smitten with a curse unless there is a welding link of some kind or other between the fathers and the children. . . . We without [our dead] cannot be made perfect; neither can they without us be made perfect. . . . [This] dispensation is now beginning to usher in, that a whole and complete and perfect union, and welding together of dispensations, and keys, and powers, and glories should take place" (D&C 128:18).

"Jesus wants me for a sunbeam"?[16] Yes! And you too! He also wants us as bonding blacksmiths—creating celestial welding links—to curb the curse (D&C 27:9; 110:14–15; 128:18; 138:48) of family fragmentation. The earth was created and temples provided so that families can be together forever (D&C 2:2–3; 132:19; 138:47–48; Joseph Smith—History 1:39).

Many, if not most, of us could repent and be converted to more temple and family history work for our ancestors. Thus, our repentance is necessary and essential for their repentance.

For all our kindred dead, to the twenty-eight-year-old woman mired in the swamp of sin, and to each one of us, I declare that the sweet blessing of repentance is possible. It comes through complete conversion to the Lord and His holy work.

NOTES

From a talk given at general conference, April 2007.

1. President Spencer W. Kimball described procrastination as "an unwillingness to accept personal responsibilities *now*" (*Teachings of Presidents of the Church: Spencer W. Kimball* [Salt Lake City: The Church of Jesus Christ of Latter-day Saints, 2006], 4).
2. We also remember the sinful people under the care of their concerned leader, Mormon, who wrote, "I was without hope, for I knew the judgments of the Lord which should come upon them; for they repented not of their iniquities, but did struggle for their lives without calling upon that Being who created them" (Mormon 5:2).
3. Especially in these latter days.
4. "The first principles and ordinances of the Gospel are: first, Faith in the Lord Jesus Christ; second, Repentance; third, Baptism by immersion for the remission of sins; fourth, Laying on of hands for the gift of the Holy Ghost" (Articles of Faith 1:4; see also D&C 39:6; 84:27; 138:19).
5. Another example is "I have given you the law and the commandments of my Father, that ye shall believe in me, and that ye shall repent of your sins, and come unto me with a broken heart and a contrite spirit" (3 Nephi 12:19).
6. *Webster's Ninth New Collegiate Dictionary* (1987), "repent," 999.
7. If no other person has been offended, confession should be prayerfully offered to God. He who hears in secret may reward openly (Matthew 6:4, 6, 18; 3 Nephi 13:4, 6, 18).
8. In the minds of some people, the word *repent* also conjures up terms like *penalty* and *penalize,* which connote punishment. If they are not guilty of punishable sin, they may reason that they have no need to repent.
9. President Spencer W. Kimball said: "There is a prevalent, perhaps subconscious, feeling that the Lord designed repentance only for those who commit murder or adultery or theft or other heinous crimes. This is of course not so. If we are humble and desirous of living the gospel we will come to think of repentance as applying to everything we do in life, whether it be spiritual or temporal in nature. Repentance is for every soul who has not yet reached perfection" (*Teachings of Presidents of the Church: Spencer W. Kimball,* 37; see also 1 John 1:8; Mosiah 4:29–30).

10. *Metanoeo* was used in the Greek text of the Lord's statements in Matthew 4:17, Mark 1:15, and Luke 13:3. The same term was used by Peter in Acts 2:38, 3:19, and 8:22.

11. In Matthew 17:2 and Mark 9:2, *transfigured* was translated from *metamorphoo,* meaning "change of form."

12. In Ephesians 4:23, *mind* was translated from the Greek *nous.*

13. In Luke 1:77, Romans 2:20, and 2 Corinthians 6:6, *knowledge* was translated from *gnos* or *gnosis. Gnos,* when preceded by the negative indicator *a,* means "lack of knowledge," as in *agnostic.* In Acts 17:23, *unknown* was translated from *agnostos,* and *ignorantly* was translated from *agnoeo.*

14. In Matthew 12:18 and Romans 8:5, *spirit* was translated from the Greek *pneuma.*

15. In Acts 17:25, *breath* was translated from the Greek *pnoe.*

16. *Children's Songbook* (Salt Lake City: The Church of Jesus Christ of Latter-day Saints, 1989), 60.

14

Worthy Music: A Source of Power and Protection

Through music we raise our voices in powerful praise and prayer. Hymns provide a pattern of worship that is pleasing to God. He taught us through the Prophet Brigham Young to "praise the Lord with singing, with music, . . . and with a prayer of praise and thanksgiving" (D&C 136:28).

Who can help but be moved by the lyrics in a hymn such as "When I Survey the Wondrous Cross," by English poet Isaac Watts? The message focuses on the Atonement of Jesus Christ:

> *When I survey the wondrous cross,*
> *On which the Prince of glory died,*
> *My richest gain I count but loss,*
> *And pour contempt on all my pride.*
>
> *Forbid it, Lord! that I should boast,*
> *Save in the death of Christ my God:*

All the vain things that charm me most,
I sacrifice them to His blood. . . .

Were the whole realm of nature mine,
That were a present far too small;
Love so amazing, so divine,
Demands my soul, my life, my all.[1]

Indeed, Isaac Watts did demand much from himself. In his lifetime he wrote approximately six hundred hymns. Two of his most productive years were between his graduation from school at age twenty and his taking a job teaching when he was twenty-two. At that young age many great hymns flowed from him. Lyrics by Isaac Watts in the LDS hymnbook include "Joy to the World," "Sweet Is the Work," and "He Died! The Great Redeemer Died."[2]

Even as a small boy, Isaac had poetic potential. "Once during family prayers, he began to laugh. His father asked him why. [Isaac] replied that he had heard a sound and opened his eyes to see a mouse climbing a rope in a corner, and had immediately thought,

"A little mouse for want of stairs

"ran up a rope to say its prayers.

"His father thought this irreverent, and proceeded to administer [physical] punishment, in the midst of which Isaac called out,

"Father, father, mercy take,

"and I will no more verses make."[3]

I would like to comment on another song in our hymnbook. The text of "How Great Thou Art" was written by a young minister in Sweden named Carl Gustav Boberg when he was only twenty-five years old. After attending a church meeting, he walked two miles along the southeastern coast of Sweden in a thunderstorm. The experience inspired him to write the words, which were later translated into English by Stuart K. Hine:

> *O Lord my God, when I in awesome wonder*
> *Consider all the worlds thy hands have made,*
> *I see the stars, I hear the rolling thunder,*
> *Thy pow'r thru-out the universe displayed;*
> *Then sings my soul, my Savior God, to thee,*
> *How great thou art! How great thou art!*[4]

On one occasion I was in a mission conference when a missionary, with great compassion and with tears in his eyes, asked me, "Why did the Savior have to suffer so much?" I reached for our hymnbook, turned to this song, and answered his question with this verse:

> *And when I think that God, his Son not sparing,*
> *Sent him to die, I scarce can take it in,*
> *That on the cross, my burden gladly bearing,*
> *He bled and died to take away my sin.*[5]

Jesus suffered so much because of His love for you and me. What a message! Worthy music is powerful. It has power to make us humble, prayerful, and grateful.

Prophets through all generations have taught the importance of worthy music in expressions of worship, which a few citations from the scriptures may serve to illustrate. An Old Testament scripture bids us to "make a joyful noise unto the Lord, all the earth: make a loud noise, and rejoice, and sing praise" (Psalm 98:4). In the Hebrew language, those words literally mean to *burst* forth into song and to *shout* for joy. Contrast that spirit of enthusiasm with scenes we may see at church when some Latter-day Saints sing only passively and without a spirit of joy.

A New Testament scripture counsels you and me to have a well of good music within:

"Speaking to yourselves in psalms and hymns and spiritual songs, singing and making melody in your heart to the Lord; giving thanks always for all things unto God and the Father in the name of our Lord Jesus Christ" (Ephesians 5:19–20).

Another New Testament verse says, "Let the word of Christ dwell in you . . . ; teaching and admonishing one another in psalms and hymns and spiritual songs, singing with grace in your hearts to the Lord" (Colossians 3:1).

From the New Testament we also learn that the Lord and His Apostles sang a hymn at the Last Supper (Matthew 26:30). That tradition continues in our day. Each time members of the First Presidency and the Quorum of the Twelve Apostles meet in the temple, we begin with a hymn. It sets a sweet, spiritual tone for our deliberations.

The Book of Mormon teaches that our desire to sing praises to the Lord comes with our complete conversion to Him. Alma made this penetrating statement: "I say unto you, my brethren, if ye have experienced a change of heart, and if ye have felt to sing the song of redeeming love, I would ask, can ye feel so now?" (Alma 5:26).

Ammon later exclaimed, "Blessed be the name of our God; let us sing to his praise, yea, let us give thanks to his holy name, for he doth work righteousness forever" (Alma 26:8).

Complete conversion is the key to our experiencing God's greatest blessings. In the Doctrine and Covenants, we read this expression from the Lord: "For my soul delighteth in the song of the heart; yea, the song of the righteous is a prayer unto me, and it shall be answered with a blessing upon their heads" (D&C 25:12).

In the preface to our hymnbook, the First Presidency has provided this statement:

"Inspirational music is an essential part of our church meetings. The hymns invite the Spirit of the Lord, create a feeling of reverence, unify us as members, and provide a way for us to offer praises to the Lord.

"Some of the greatest sermons are preached by the singing of hymns. Hymns move us to repentance and good works, build testimony and faith, comfort the weary, console the mourning, and inspire us to endure to the end.

"We hope to see an increase of hymn singing in our congregations. We encourage all members, whether musically inclined or not, to join with us in singing the hymns. We hope leaders, teachers, and members who are called on to speak will turn often to the hymnbook to find sermons presented powerfully and beautifully in verse. . . .

" . . . Latter-day Saints should fill their homes with the sound of worthy music. . . .

"Hymns can also help us withstand the temptations of the adversary. We encourage you to memorize your favorite hymns and study the scriptures that relate to them. Then, if unworthy thoughts enter your mind, sing a hymn to yourself, crowding out the evil with the good."[6]

Worthy music also has the power to persuade. We learn this lesson from the writings of John Jaques. He was born in England in 1827, a son of Wesleyan Methodist parents. In his youth John earnestly sought the true religion. He studied intensively with Latter-day Saint missionaries and, at the age of eighteen, became a member of The Church of Jesus Christ of Latter-day Saints.

"John's austere father, upset upon hearing this news, wrote: 'I wished you . . . to attend the Wesleyan Chapel. They [the Mormons] do not teach you . . . [to] honor and obey your parents. I . . . hope you will give up the idea of belonging to such a party. . . . It is fiction.'

"John's reply, written March 14, 1847, when he was but twenty years of age, included these words: 'Dear Father: I would pray . . . that I may understand the things of the Kingdom of God and carry my ideas to you. . . . Since I [joined the Church] my eyes have been opened, and I have been able to understand the truth. I can bear testimony to the truth . . . of the doctrines . . . in the Church of Jesus Christ of Latter-day Saints.'"[7]

Three years later, at age twenty-three, John wrote the words to a hymn that we know and love:

> *Oh say, what is truth? 'Tis the fairest gem*
> *That the riches of worlds can produce,*
> *And priceless the value of truth will be when*
> *The proud monarch's costliest diadem*
> *Is counted but dross and refuse.*
>
> *Yes, say, what is truth? 'Tis the brightest prize*
> *To which mortals or Gods can aspire.*
> *Go search in the depths where it glittering lies,*
> *Or ascend in pursuit to the loftiest skies:*
> *'Tis an aim for the noblest desire.*
>
> *The sceptre may fall from the despot's grasp*
> *When with winds of stern justice he copes.*
> *But the pillar of truth will endure to the last,*
> *And its firm-rooted bulwarks outstand the rude blast*
> *And the wreck of the fell tyrant's hopes.*
>
> *Then say, what is truth? 'Tis the last and the first,*
> *For the limits of time it steps o'er.*
> *Tho the heavens depart and the earth's fountains burst,*
> *Truth, the sum of existence, will weather the worst,*
> *Eternal, unchanged, evermore.*[8]

John stood firm in his conviction of the truth. He remained true and faithful and ultimately served as assistant to the Church historian from 1889 until his death on June 1, 1900.

Music has a sweet power to promote unity and love in the family. Not only is it an important component of family home evening, but it can also exert a continuing influence for good well beyond times when children are small. For my gift to the family one Christmas, I prepared a compact-disc recording of musical memories. I sat at the piano and recorded a variety of songs that I had sung or played to the children through the years. They liked it. Some of the grandchildren told me that the CD was "cool."

Many of us have the opportunity to influence music that is selected for church services. A few thoughts may be helpful to us in using that influence. Remember, music has power to provide spiritual nourishment.[9] It has healing power.[10] It has power to facilitate worship; it allows us to contemplate the Atonement and the Restoration of the gospel with its saving principles and exalting ordinances. Music provides power for us to express prayerful thoughts and bear testimony of sacred truths.

Music has power to overcome language barriers. In my experience, some of the most moving congregational singing has been rendered in languages that are foreign to me. Yet it spoke strongly to my soul.

The purpose of music in our church services is not for performance but for worship. Prayerfully selected compositions and excellent performances are appropriate in our worship services when and if members feel a spirit of worship and revelation. Church music should support the Lord and His work and not attract attention to itself.

Protection

Worthy music not only has power, but it can also provide protection. For many years President Boyd K. Packer has taught this concept. He has often quoted a statement issued by the First Presidency many years ago: "Music can be used to exalt and inspire or to carry messages of degradation and destruction. It is therefore important that as Latter-day Saints we at all times apply the principles of the gospel and seek the guidance of the Spirit in selecting the music with which we surround ourselves."[11]

Wherever we are, we should carefully choose what we see and hear. Some of you would not knowingly tolerate pornography in your homes, yet you would allow music into your lives that can be just as devastating.

Many youth listen to music that can be described as loud and fast, becoming louder and faster. It aims to agitate, not to pacify; to excite more than to calm. Beware of that kind of music.

As you know, continued exposure to loud sounds will, in time, damage delicate organs of hearing. In like manner, if you overindulge in loud music, you will more likely become spiritually deaf. You may not be able to hear the still, small voice. A scripture states, "The Lord your God . . . hath spoken unto you in a still small voice, but ye were past feeling, that ye could not feel his words" (1 Nephi 17:45).

Do not degrade yourself with the numbing shabbiness and irreverence of music that is not worthy of you. Delete the rubbish from your minds and your iPods. Protect your personal standards! Be selective! Be wise!

Do not allow unworthy, raucous music to enter your life. It is not harmless. It can weaken your defense and allow unworthy thoughts into your mind and pave the way to unworthy acts. Please remember:

"That which [does] not edify is not of God, and is darkness.

"That which is of God is light" (D&C 50:23–24).

Please fill your minds with worthy sights and sounds. Cultivate your precious gift of the Holy Ghost. Protect it as the priceless gift that it is. Carefully listen for its quiet communication. You will be spiritually stronger if you do. You know the proverb "As [a man] thinketh in his heart, so is he" (Proverbs 23:7). As you control your thoughts, you control your actions. Indeed, worthy music can provide power and protection for your soul.

I close with the lyrics from the hymn "Our Prayer to Thee."¹² I wrote the words as my prayerful feelings for our Father in Heaven:

> *We pray to Thee, our Heavenly Father,*
> *With grateful hearts and fond emotion.*
> *We thank Thee for our great Exemplar—*
> *Thy beloved and atoning Son—*
> *Who gave Himself as sacred ransom,*
> *That we could live again with Thee!*
> *Our joy is full, our song so gladsome;*
> *Renew our faith and hope in Thee.*
>
> *We pray to Thee, our Heavenly Father,*
> *With thankful hearts and adoration.*
> *We thank Thee for our loving Savior,*
> *Who redeemed us from death and sin;*
> *He gave to us His truth to brighten*
> *Our path, to help us walk His way,*

To love and serve, to lift and lighten
The lives of all who will obey.

We pray to Thee, our Heavenly Father,
With gratitude and deep devotion
For loving faith and endless splendor—
Eternal glory—bound as one!
We pray for mercy and forgiveness
And hope to know Thy holy will.
We yearn for Thee, we plead in meekness,
Thy trust in us may we fulfill.

NOTES

From a Church Educational System fireside address, May 2008.

1. B. B. McKinney, ed., *The Broadman Hymnal* (Nashville, TN: The Broadman Press, 1940), no. 191.
2. *Hymns* (Salt Lake City: The Church of Jesus Christ of Latter-day Saints, 1985), nos. 201, 147, 192.
3. "Isaac Watts, hymn-writer," http://elvis.rowan.edu/~kilroy/JEK/11/25c.html.
4. "How Great Thou Art," *Hymns,* no. 86; see footnote in the hymnal regarding the author's original words.
5. *Hymns,* no. 86.
6. *Hymns,* ix–x.
7. Russell M. Nelson, *The Power within Us* (Salt Lake City: Deseret Book, 1988), 90–91; see Stella Jaques Bell, *Life History and Writings of John Jaques* (Rexburg, ID: Ricks College Press, 1978), 19–21.
8. "Oh Say, What Is Truth?" *Hymns,* no. 272.
9. See Jay E. Jensen, "The Nourishing Power of Hymns," *Ensign,* May 2007, 11–13.
10. See "The Healing Power of Hymns," *Ensign,* April 2008, 66–69.
11. *Priesthood Bulletin,* December 1970, 20; *Priesthood Bulletin,* August 1973, 4; quoted in Boyd K. Packer, "Inspiring Music—Worthy Thoughts," *Ensign,* January 1974, 25.
12. In Russell M. Nelson, "Sweet Hour of Prayer," *Ensign,* May 2003, 9; both words and music are found inside the back cover of this issue.

15

The Magnificence of Man

I invite you to ponder things magnificent. The word *magnif-icent* is derived from two Latin roots. The prefix *magni* comes from a term meaning "great." The suffix comes from the Latin *facere,* which means "to make" or "to do." A simple definition of *magnificent,* then, might be "great deed" or "greatly made."

Think of the most magnificent sight you have ever seen. It could be a meadow in springtime filled with beautiful wild-flowers. Or perhaps you have been awestruck, as have I, at the magnificence of a single rose with its special beauty and perfume. I have come to appreciate the magnificence of an orange, with each droplet of juice neatly packaged in an edible container, joined with many other packets, grouped in sections, and all neatly wrapped in a disposable, biodegradable peel.

Some would say that the most magnificent sight they have

ever beheld is the heavens on a summer night, with stars beyond number dotting the sky. Those who have traveled in orbit through space say that their view of the planet Earth is one of the most magnificent sights they have ever observed.

Some might choose the view of the Grand Canyon at sunrise; others, the beauty of a mountain lake, river, waterfall, or desert.

Some might select a peacock with its tail in full fan or a handsome horse. Others would nominate the beauty of butterfly wings or a hummingbird seemingly suspended in midair while feeding.

These magnificent sights are wondrous beyond measure. They are all "great deeds" of our divine Creator.

Now ponder the magnificence of all that is portrayed when you look in the mirror. Ignore the freckles, unruly hair, or blemishes, and look beyond to see the real you—a child of God—created by Him in His image. Looking beyond the surface you see in the mirror, open the treasure chest to understanding the marvelous attributes of your body and discover, at least in part, the magnificence of man. Here are some of the glittering jewels of magnificence in this treasure chest.

The Human Embryo

In the first compartment of the treasure chest, we might look at the magnificence of our creation itself.

We don't know precisely how two germ cells unite to become a human embryo, but we do know that both the female cell and the male cell contain all of the new individual's hereditary material and information, stored in a space so small it cannot be seen by the naked eye. Twenty-three chromosomes from both the father and the mother unite in one new cell. These chromosomes contain thousands of genes. A marvelous process of genetic coding is established by which all the basic human characteristics of the unborn person are determined. A new DNA complex is thus formed. A continuum of growth is instituted that results in a new human being.

Approximately twenty-two days after two germ cells have united, a little heart begins to beat. At twenty-six days the circulation of blood begins. Cells multiply, divide, and become differentiated. Some become eyes that see; others become ears that hear; while still others are destined to become fingers that feel the wonderful things about us. Yes, awareness of the magnificence of man begins with the miracles of our conception and creation.

Specific Organs

In our treasure chest of understanding, we can look to the compartment that contains the capability of selected organs. Each jewel merits admiration, appreciation, and awe.

Let us mention first the magnificence of the eyes with which we see. No doubt you have stood before the mirror and watched the pupils of your eyes react to changes in the intensity of light, dilating to let in more light and constricting to reduce the light allowed to reach the sensitive retina of the eye. A self-focusing lens is at the front of each eye. Nerves and muscles synchronize the function of two separate eyes to produce one three-dimensional image. Eyes are connected to the brain, ready to record sights seen. No cords, no batteries, no external connections are needed; our visual apparatus is marvelous—infinitely more priceless than any camera that money can buy.

While we may admire good stereophonic equipment for sensing sound, ponder by comparison the magnificence of the human ear. It is truly remarkable. Compacted into an area about the size of a marble is all the equipment needed to perceive sound. A tiny tympanic membrane serves as the diaphragm. Minute ossicles amplify the signal, which is transmitted along nerve lines to the brain. The brain then registers the result of hearing. This marvelous sound system is also connected to the recording instrument of the brain.

A large portion of my life's study and research has been focused on the jewel of the human heart—a pump that is so magnificent that its power is almost beyond our comprehension. To control the direction of the flow of blood within it, there are four important valves, pliable as a parachute and delicate as a silk scarf. They open and close more than one hundred thousand times a day—more than thirty-six million times a year. Yet, unless altered by disease, they are so rugged that they stand this kind of wear seemingly indefinitely. No man-made material developed thus far can be flexed this frequently and for so long without breaking.

The amount of work done by the heart is truly amazing. Each day it pumps enough fluid to fill a 2,000-gallon tank car. The work it performs daily is equivalent to lifting a 150-pound man to the top of the Empire State Building, while consuming only about four watts of energy—less than that used to power a small lightbulb.

At the crest of the heart is an electrical generator that transmits energy down special lines, causing myriad muscle fibers to beat in coordination and in rhythm. This synchrony would be the envy of the conductor of any orchestra.

All this power is condensed in this faithful pump—the

human heart—about the size of one's fist, energized from within by an endowment from on high.

One of the most wondrous of all jewels in this treasure chest is the human brain with its intricate combination of power cells, recording, memory, storage, and retrieval systems. It serves as headquarters for the personality and character of each human being. As I observe the lives of great individuals, I sense that the capacity of the brain is seemingly infinite. Wise men can become even wiser as each experience builds upon previous experience. Indeed, continuing exercise of the intellect brings forth increased intellectual capacity.

While I marvel at a computer and admire the work it can do, I respect even more the mind of man, which developed the computer. The human brain is certainly a recording instrument that will participate in our judgment one day when we stand before the Lord. The Book of Mormon speaks of a "bright recollection" (Alma 11:43) and of a "perfect remembrance" (Alma 5:18) that will be with us at that time. Each one of us carries that recording instrument guarded within the vault of the human skull.

As we symbolically sift through the treasure chest of understanding, we could spend hours, even a lifetime, studying the incredible chemical capacity of the liver, the kidneys, and all of the endocrine and exocrine glands of the body. Each is a shimmering jewel, worthy of our study and our deepest gratitude.

Other Jewels

Now let us turn our attention to jewels in another compartment in the treasure chest of understanding, as we consider some concepts that bridge beyond individual organ systems.

1. The first concept is that of *reserve,* or *backup.* In the theater, major actors often have understudies for backup. In electrical instruments, backup in the event of power failure may be provided by batteries. In the body, backup is provided by a number of organs that are paired, such as eyes, ears, lungs, adrenal glands, kidneys, and more. In the event of illness, injury, or loss of one of these organs, the other is ready to keep our bodily functions intact. In the event of loss of sight or hearing altogether, other sensory powers become augmented in a miraculous manner.

Some backup systems are not so apparent. For example, crucial single organs, such as the brain, the heart, and the liver, have a double blood supply. They are all nourished by two routes of circulation that minimize damage in the event of loss of blood flow through any single blood vessel.

Another dimension of backup I will describe as *collateral pathways.* For example, if your nasal passageways are obstructed by a "stuffy nose," you may breathe through your mouth. Similarly, collateral pathways may grow if blood vessels or nerves are obstructed or severed.

2. Consider another concept, that of *self-defense* of the body. One day I watched some three-year-old children lapping water from the sidewalk after it had overflowed through a neighbor's garden. I suppose the germs they ingested were incalculable in number, but not one of those children became ill. They were defended by their bodies. As soon as that dirty drink reached their stomach, hydrochloric acid went to work to purify the water and protect the lives of those innocent children.

Think of the protection provided by the skin. Could you make or even conjure in your mind how to create a cloak that would protect you and, at the same time, warn you against injuries from excessive heat or cold? That is what the skin does.

It even gives signals indicating that another part of the body is ailing. The skin can flush and sweat with fever. When a person is frightened or ill, the skin pales. When a person is embarrassed, the skin blushes. And it is replete with nerve fibers that communicate and often limit possible harm through perception of pain.

Pain itself is part of the body's defense mechanism. For example, sensory areas of the mouth guard and protect the esophagus, which is delicate and has few nerve fibers. Like a sentinel, the mouth receives warnings if drinks are too hot and protects the esophagus from becoming burned.

The body's defenses include chemical antibodies that are manufactured in response to infections. Each time a person is exposed to a bacterial or viral infection, the body produces antibodies that not only combat that infection but also persist with memory to strengthen resistance in days to come. When military conscription was required during World War II, soldiers who had come from isolated rural areas had much less immunity and were more prone to infections than were those who had come from more highly populated urban areas and whose resistance was subsequently better developed.

3. Closely related to the concept of self-defense is that of *self-repair*. Consider the fact that broken bones mend and become strong once again. If we were to break one of the legs of a chair, how long would we have to wait for that chair leg to heal itself? It would never happen. Yet many people today walk on legs that once were broken. Lacerations in the skin heal themselves. A leak in the circulation will seal itself, a power that circulatory systems outside the body do not have. I gained appreciation for this fact early in my research career while working in the laboratory to create an artificial heart-lung machine. Whenever tubing in that machine would spring a leak, I could

count on spending long hours cleaning up the lab and coming home late for dinner. Never did a leak in the artificial heart-lung machine ever seal itself.

4. Another remarkable concept is that of *self-renewal.* Each cell in the body is created and then regenerated from elements of the earth according to the recipe or formula contained within genes unique to the individual. The average red blood corpuscle, for example, lives about one hundred twenty days and then dies and is replaced by another. Each time we bathe, thousands of dead and dying cells are scrubbed away, to be replaced by a younger crop.

5. Also in our treasure chest is the concept of *autoregulation.* Have you ever wondered why you can't swim under water very long? Autoregulation limits the time you can hold your breath. As breath is held, carbon dioxide accumulates. Partial pressure of carbon dioxide is monitored continuously by two carotid bodies in the neck, which transmit signals up nerves to the brain. The brain then sends stimuli to muscles of respiration, causing them to work so that we inhale a new refreshment of oxygen and eliminate retained carbon dioxide.

And have you ever wondered why you can tolerate extremes of hot and cold weather? Despite wide fluctuations in the temperature of man's environment, the temperature of each person's body is carefully controlled within certain very narrow bounds.

These are but two of many servomechanisms that autoregulate individual ingredients in our bodies. The number of these systems exceeds our ability to enumerate them. Sodium, potassium, water, glucose, protein, nitrogen are but a few of the many constituents continuously monitored by chemical regulators within our bodies.

6. Consider now the concept of *adaptation.* People on the earth dwell amidst climatic and dietary differences of vast

scope. Eskimos in the Arctic Circle consume a diet with a large component of fat, which is acceptable and even necessary to sustain life in a very cold climate. Polynesians, on the other hand, eat a diet provided by a tropical environment. Yet these different groups work and adapt to varying conditions and diet available to them.

7. The concept of *identity* in reproduction is marvelous to contemplate. Each of us possesses seeds that carry our unique chromosomes and genes that help determine specific cellular identity for our children. For this reason, tissues surgically transplanted from one person to another can survive only if the host's immune response, which clearly recognizes tissues foreign to the inherited genetic formula, is suppressed. Truly we are blessed with power to have children born in the likeness of parents.

An Interesting Paradox

As we consider self-defense, self-repair, and self-renewal, an interesting paradox emerges. Limitless life could result if these marvelous qualities of the body continued in perpetuity. If we could create anything that could defend itself, repair itself, and renew itself without limit, we could create perpetual life. That is what our Creator did with the bodies He created for Adam and Eve in the Garden of Eden. Had they continued to be nourished from the tree of life, they would have lived forever. According to the Lord, as revealed through His prophets, the fall of Adam instituted the aging process, which results ultimately in physical death. Of course, we do not understand all the chemistry, but we are witnesses of the consequences of growing old. This and other pathways of release assure that there is a limit to the length of life upon the earth.

Yes, troubles do develop in bodies that do not repair themselves with time. To the skilled physician, this profound question is posed by each sick patient seen: Will this illness get better or worse with the passage of time? If the former, then all that is needed is supportive care. If the latter, then significant help is needed to convert the process of progressive deterioration to one that might improve with time.

When death comes, it generally seems to the mortal mind to be untimely. At such times we need to have the larger view that death is part of life. Alma tells us, "It was not expedient that man should be reclaimed from this temporal death, for that would destroy the great plan of happiness" (Alma 42:8; see also D&C 29:43).

When severe illness or tragic injury claim an individual in the flowering prime of life, we can take comfort in this fact: the very laws that could not allow life to persist here are the same eternal laws that will be implemented at the time of the resurrection, when the body "shall be restored to [its] proper and perfect frame" (Alma 40:23).

Our Divine Creation

Thoughts of life, death, and resurrection bring us to face crucial questions. How were we made? By whom? And why?

Through the ages, some persons without scriptural understanding have tried to explain our existence by pretentious words such as *ex nihilo* (out of nothing). Others have deduced that, because of certain similarities between different forms of life, there has been a natural selection of the species, or organic evolution from one form to another. Still others have concluded that man came as a consequence of a "big bang," which resulted in the creation of our planet and life upon it.

To me, such theories are unbelievable. Could an explosion in a printing shop produce a dictionary? It's unthinkable! One might argue that it is within a remote realm of possibility, but even if that could happen, such a dictionary could certainly not heal its own torn pages, renew its own worn corners, or reproduce its own subsequent editions.

We are children of God, created by Him and formed in His image. Recently I studied the scriptures simply to find how many times they testify of the divine creation of man. Looking up references that referred to either *create* or *form* (or their derivatives) with *man* (or such derivatives as *men, male, woman,* or *female*) in the same verse, I found that at least fifty-five passages of scripture attest to our divine creation. I have selected one to represent all those verses that convey the same conclusion: "The Gods took counsel among themselves and said: Let us go down and form man in our image, after our likeness. . . . So the Gods went down to organize man in their own image, in the image of the Gods to form they him, male and female to form they them" (Abraham 4:26–27).

I believe all of those scriptures pertaining to the creation of man. But the decision to believe is a spiritual one, not born solely by an understanding of things physical: "The natural man receiveth not the things of the Spirit of God: for they are foolishness unto him: neither can he know them, because they are spiritually discerned" (1 Corinthians 2:14).

It is incumbent upon each informed and spiritually attuned person to help overcome such foolishness by those who would deny divine creation or think that mankind simply evolved. By the Spirit, we perceive the truer and more believable wisdom of God.

With great conviction I add my testimony to that of my fellow apostle Paul, who said: "Know ye not that ye are the temple of God, and that the Spirit of God dwelleth in you? If any man defile the temple of God, him shall God destroy; for the temple of God is holy, which temple ye are" (1 Corinthians 3:16–17).

The Lord has said that "the spirit and the body are the soul of man" (D&C 88:15). Each of us, therefore, is a dual being—a biological (physical) entity and an intellectual (spiritual) entity. The combination of both is intimate throughout mortality.

In the beginning, man, as that intellectual entity, was with God. Our intelligence was not created or made; nor can it be (D&C 93:29).

That spirit, joined with a physical body of such remarkable qualities, becomes a living soul of supernal worth. The psalmist so expressed this thought: "When I consider thy heavens, the work of thy fingers, the moon and the stars, which thou hast ordained; what is man, that thou art mindful of him? . . . For thou hast made him a little lower than the angels, and hast crowned him with glory and honour" (Psalm 8:3–5).

Why were we created? Why are we here? Why are we upon the earth?

God has made it plain over and over again that the world was made for mankind to exist. We are here to work out our divine destiny, according to an eternal plan presented to us in the great council of heaven. Our bodies have been created to accommodate our spirits, to allow us to experience the challenges of mortality.

With this understanding, it is pure sacrilege to let anything enter the body that might defile this physical temple of God. It is irreverent to let even the gaze of our precious eyesight, or the sensors of our touch or hearing, supply the brain with memories that are unclean or unworthy.

Could any of us lightly regard precious seeds of reproduction—specifically and uniquely ours—or disregard the moral laws of God, who gave divine rules governing their sacred use?

Knowing that we are created as children of God and that He has given us agency to choose, we must also know that we are accountable to Him. He has defined the truth and has prescribed commandments. Obedience to His law brings us joy. Disobedience of His commandments is sin and brings unhappiness. While we live in a world that seems increasingly reluctant to designate dishonorable deeds as sinful, a scripture warns us: "Fools make a mock at sin: but among the righteous there is favour" (Proverbs 14:9).

No one is perfect. Some may have sinned grievously in transgressing God's laws. Mercifully, we can repent. That is an important part of life's opportunities as well.

Repentance requires spiritual dominion over appetites of the flesh. Every physical system has appetite. Our desires to eat, drink, see, hear, and feel respond to those appetites. But all appetites must be controlled by the intellect for us to attain true joy. On the other hand, whenever we allow uncontrolled appetites of the body to determine behavior opposed to nobler promptings of the Spirit, the stage is set for misery and grief.

Substances such as alcohol, tobacco, and harmful drugs are forbidden by the Lord. We have similarly been warned about the evils of pornography and unclean thoughts. Appetites for these degrading forces can become addictive. Physical or mental addictions become doubly serious because, in time, they enslave both the body and the spirit.

When we truly know our divine nature, our thoughts and

behavior will be more appropriate. Then we will control our appetites. We will focus our eyes on sights, our ears on sounds, and our minds on thoughts that are a credit to our physical creation as a temple of our Father in Heaven.

In daily prayer we may gratefully acknowledge God as our Creator and thank Him for the magnificence of our physical temple. Then we must heed His counsel.

More Yet to Learn

Though we cannot fully comprehend the magnificence of man, in faith we can continue our reverent quest. We may join with Jacob in this marvelous declaration: "Behold, great and marvelous are the works of the Lord. How unsearchable are the depths of the mysteries of him; and it is impossible that man should find out all his ways. . . . For behold, by the power of his word man came upon the face of the earth, which earth was created by the power of his word. . . . Therefore, brethren, seek not to counsel the Lord, but to take counsel from his hand" (Jacob 4:8–10).

For years I have attended scientific meetings of learned societies. Medical scientists and practitioners by the thousands participate in such assemblies annually from all over the world. The quest for knowledge is endless. It seems that the more we know, the more there is yet to learn. It is impossible that any of us may learn all the ways of God. But as we are faithful and are deeply rooted in scriptural accounts of God's magnificent creations, we will be well prepared for future discoveries. All truth is compatible because it all emanates from God.

Of course, we know that "there is an opposition in all things" (2 Nephi 2:11). In the world even many so-called "educators" teach contrary to divine truth. Be mindful of this prophetic counsel: "O the vainness, and the frailties, and the foolishness of men! When they are learned they think they are wise, and they hearken not unto the counsel of God, for they set it aside, supposing they know of themselves, wherefore, their wisdom is foolishness and it profiteth them not. And they shall perish. But to be learned is good if they hearken unto the counsels of God" (2 Nephi 9:28–29).

We need not be reminded that the work and glory of the Lord are opposed by forces of Satan, who is the master of deceit. Many follow his teachings. Remember, "Man may deceive his fellow-men, deception may follow deception, and the children of the wicked one may have power to seduce the foolish and untaught, till naught but fiction feeds the many, and the fruit of falsehood carries in its current the giddy to the grave" (Joseph Smith–History 1:71 note).

Be wise and keep away from temptations and snares. Cautiously avoid "foolish and hurtful lusts, which drown men in destruction and perdition. . . . Flee these things; and follow after righteousness, godliness, faith, love, patience, meekness. Fight the good fight of faith, lay hold on eternal life" (1 Timothy 6:9, 11–12).

Our Eternal Spirit

The magnificence of man is matchless. Remember, glorious as this physical tabernacle is, the body is designed to support something even more glorious—the eternal spirit that dwells in the mortal frame of each of us. The great accomplishments of this life are rarely physical. Those attributes by which we will be judged one day are spiritual. With the blessing of our bodies to assist us, we may develop spiritual qualities of honesty, integrity, compassion, and love. Only with the development of the spirit may we acquire "faith, virtue, knowledge, temperance, patience, brotherly kindness, godliness, charity, humility, [and] diligence" (D&C 4:6).

May we pattern our lives after our great Exemplar, even Jesus the Christ, whose parting words among mankind included this eternal challenge: "What manner of men ought ye to be? . . . even as I am" (3 Nephi 27:27). We are sons and daughters of God. He is our Father; we are His children. Our divine inheritance is the magnificence of man.

NOTE

From a talk given at Brigham Young University, March 1987.

16

Reflection and Resolution

If I had the wish of my heart, I would welcome a private hour with every person, particularly every young adult, who may be reading these words. I would like to hear your own reflections and then to share with you a vision of what you can become in your own special way.

I would like to provide such vision. So let's follow the pattern of the Lord, who often chose to instruct His disciples on a high mountain. He so took Moses to see the scope of the work that was ahead (Moses 1:1). To another high mountain the Lord later took Peter, James, and John (Matthew 17:1). There, power and authority, vision and purpose were given to them to qualify them for the work (Isaiah 40:9; Ezekiel 40).

I would like to share a similar vision with each of you. Let us imagine that you and I are alone together on a mountaintop.

Let's start with William. We reflect first on your accomplishments that have brought you to this point in your life. I met you as a handsome and bright elder on your mission. You rendered such wonderful service. Many people now understand the gospel because of you. Some have even joined the Church. They and their posterity will always hold your name dear to their hearts. Reflections on your mission should always give you a sense of deep satisfaction.

Now, William, what will your resolutions for your future life include? What would you like to be? Have you gone to a quiet, secluded spot to be all alone? Have you found your own "Sacred Grove" equivalent, where you can pour out the secret longings of your soul in prayer to your Father in Heaven? Have you really conversed with God as one man speaks with another? Have you declared your allegiance to Him and your availability to Him, without any reservation? Have you said, "Here I am, Lord! Use me"? As you have pled with Him, have you put behind any counterfeit clichés that may have been said in prayers of the past? Have you cleanly and completely declared your commitment to be a saint, an elder, a righteous disciple, through good times and bad? Such a resounding resolution would bring joy to your Heavenly Father.

Now I see Mary—beautiful Mary. I reflect on days when you were small and so full of fun. Now you are a woman, mature and wise.

What will you resolve in your heart to be? You will surely help your husband honor his priesthood as you share its blessings together. I already know of your commitment to chastity. It is the powerful protector of virile manhood and the crown of beautiful womanhood. You will continue in your resolve to be clean—to avoid flirtatious or flippant behavior unbecoming a lovely daughter of God.

You and your companion should resolve never to make un-complimentary comments about one another to anyone at any time. Good habit patterns are best established during courtship. Never stoop to demeaning words that hurt. Together, resolve now to make of your home a place of prayer. Make it a sanctuary of faith where servants of the Lord are always welcome and where scriptures are read and discussed together. You will both want to grow in true spiritual symmetry.

Remember, Mary, your partner's feelings about paying tithing will in a large measure be shaped by your attitude. Words of encouragement from you will help him feel confident in his commitment to tithe, especially during your early years together when pocketbooks are so thin. Be sure your bishop knows of your resolution to help build the kingdom in the fraction of the frontier where you are called upon to live.

Calls in the Church are not only opportunities to help others but are also a source of blessings in your lives. The Lord said, "Thy duty is unto the church forever, and this because of thy family" (D&C 23:3). Now is the time to make that resolution to continue to serve the Lord. God bless you, Mary and your partner, and may you always continue to be best friends.

Next I would like to visit with Natasha. Your last name is usually mispronounced because of its roots in Eastern Europe. Think of what happened in that part of the world during the historic year of 1989. Surely your reflections include gratitude for such events, not only in your country but in neighboring nations as well.

During 1989 our missionaries entered the German Democratic Republic. Hundreds of grateful converts to the Church have since been baptized. New chapels are bulging with faithful souls who have made covenants to come unto Christ. Also in 1989 native sons from the German Democratic

Republic entered the mission field to serve in England, Canada, Argentina, Chile, and the United States. The holy temple in the German Democratic Republic, dedicated in 1985, has become a beacon of faith, blessing that country and its neighboring nations.

In 1989 many Eastern European countries abolished a constitutional guarantee of communist supremacy and legalized a multiparty system with free elections. Freedom to vote is closely related to freedom of worship.

Apostolic blessings and dedicatory prayers were offered in many other countries—all evidence of the growth of the Church, not only in your area but in other parts of the world as well. Truly the hand of the Lord is apparent. He said, "I will hasten my work" (D&C 88:73), and that time of hastening is upon us.

In light of these reflections, Natasha, what will you do with your life? Keep your eye on the big picture. But while you survey large fields, cultivate small ones. Prepare to serve. Take full advantage of your opportunity for an education; it will be invaluable to you. I don't think it matters much whether you study to become a librarian, a lawyer, or a musician. Complete the course you have begun, and then God can use you to bless people with the fruits of your education.

Next, I would like to visit with Peter. As a relatively recent convert to the Church, you are so happy with the truths of the gospel that have expanded your mind. As you reflect on your past, Peter, remember that before you found the Church, you had many doubts. But your confusion departed when you discovered the fulness of the gospel. Ignorance was replaced by information and then by conviction. Next came repentance. You became converted—changed—never to return to the ways of the spiritual skeptic devoid of faith.

Your choice of career is yet a bit uncertain. That can be frustrating at times. But much more important than what you do is what you are. To be your best, will you quietly and personally resolve to remain a believer? Will you continue to nurture your faith in God? Keep your faith strong enough to defend attacks upon your religious conversion. Beware! Wherever you go, there will be clever destroyers of faith, many even masquerading as fellow believers.

Your love for research in the exact sciences is a great gift. Cultivate it. As you continue your advanced studies, resolve now, Peter, to know what you will do when confronted with ideas contrary to established doctrines of the Lord. Resolve now how you will react to those who stir up contention and contest the teachings of the prophets. Prepare now for the possibility that people of prominent status will deny their own Creator. Their skeptical teachings try to diminish the divinity of the mission of the Savior and even try to nullify the doctrine of the Atonement.

Resolve now to be steadfast. Be like Nephi of old, who did "liken all scriptures unto [himself]" (Nephi 19:23). Resolve now never to compartmentalize your faith. Faith is not to be separated from your works but is to be an integral part of your works.

May I share with you some reflections of my own. Years ago in my research career in a scientific discipline I helped to develop, I found success by applying truths gleaned from the scriptures. Let me explain.

When I started medical school, we were taught that we must not touch the heart, for if we did it would stop beating. But later I pondered the scripture that tells us that "all kingdoms have a law given; . . . and unto every kingdom is given a law; and unto every law there are certain bounds also and conditions" (D&C 88:36, 38). I also pondered the scripture that certifies that "when we obtain any blessing from God, it is by obedience to that law upon which it is predicated" (D&C 130:21).

With these scriptures in mind, I concentrated on the "kingdom" of and the blessing of the beating heart. I knew that the function of even this vital organ was predicated upon law. I reasoned that if laws applicable could be understood and controlled, perhaps they could be harnessed ultimately for the healing of the sick.

To me, this meant that if we worked, studied, and asked the proper questions in our scientific experiments, we would be blessed to learn the laws that govern the beating of the heart.

In 1949 our team of researchers presented at the American College of Surgeons the report of the first successful use of an artificial heart-lung machine. It had sustained the life of an animal for thirty minutes without the animal's own heart powering its circulation.

In the decade of the 1950s, successes in the laboratory with animals were extended to human beings. Today, many of those laws governing the heart have been learned. As a result, delicate repairs are performed on damaged valves and vessels. The heartbeat can be temporarily turned off and then turned on again— provided the laws are obeyed upon which that blessing is predicated. Hundreds of thousands of open-heart operations are now performed throughout the world every year, thereby extending life for many. But you should know that it was through understanding gained from study of the scriptures, and "likening" them to this area of my interest, that I was able to make the advances I did in the field of heart surgery.

Bless you, Peter, in your desire for excellence in scientific research. Liken the scriptures to the kingdoms that pertain to your own studies. Quietly effect a warm fusion of your faith with your scholarship. Then you will have power, even the power of God, which will bless you and enlighten your way.

Next I see Dorothy. And I think I can see Dave seated beside her. You don't have plans for marriage at the moment. That day seems far, far in the future. Meanwhile, your reflections contain a mixture of both sweet and sour memories. Sweet are the happy times of your youth, but sour are the deeds of "friends" who weren't really friends after all. Some placed sordid temptations before you for which you were ill-prepared at the time. What will each of you resolve to be? Now is the time to shape your behavior to your hopes. It is not always easy. I can empathize with you.

Years ago while I served as a young intern in a large medical center, I attended a Christmas party. The host was the chief of surgery. I had made a major commitment to work for and be loyal to him and his world-famous institution, which had produced many of the great surgeons, scholars, and researchers of our generation. At the party, the chief's head resident offered alcoholic beverages to Sister Nelson and me. Of course, we politely declined.

Minutes later he returned with a more persuasive pitch: "Take a drink," he said, "or the chief will be offended." Again we declined. Our refusal infuriated the head resident. Red-faced and indignant, he said, "Nelson, you take this drink or I'll make life around here mighty miserable for you!"

I simply replied, "You do what you must, doctor, but I will do what I must." I fulfilled my promise, and he fulfilled his.

He saw to it that I had no vacation that year. His responsibility to prepare the schedule of assignments and on-call duty bore the stamp of his vitriolic vengeance against me. But now as

I reflect on this matter forty years later, I would not trade places with him today or ever.

Dorothy—and you too, Dave—remember that decisions are best made before the time of testing, whether those resolutions concern forsaking drugs, alcohol, and other addicting substances, or pornography, which can become an addiction of the mind. Resist any temptations of lust disguised as love. Instead of vice, let virtue garnish your thoughts. To all the Dorothys and Daves of the world, I urge you to choose companions well and cherish those friends who lift you and make you better in their presence. And be such friends to one another.

And now, Richard. Reflect upon your parents. They sacrificed much so you could continue to achieve. What will you resolve to be? If I can read your thoughts correctly, you are committed to strive for personal righteousness. That is a wonderful goal. But it is more difficult to measure than a goal to shed ten pounds of unwanted weight or to run or swim a measured distance. Come with me to the high mountain, and I'll suggest some ways in which you can measure your progress toward personal righteousness.

To begin, ask yourself, "What do I think of when I partake of the sacrament? Do I really concentrate on the Atonement of Jesus Christ? Do I comprehend the magnitude of His sacrifice and the magnificence of my future as I take upon myself the name of Jesus Christ and resolve to keep His commandments? As His witness, do I worthily partake of the broken bread in remembrance of His broken body? Do I worthily partake of the water, blessed and sanctified to the souls of all those who drink of it, in remembrance of His blood shed for us?"

You can recognize progress each week as you thoughtfully, regularly, and worthily partake of the sacrament.

Here's another spiritual yardstick: How do you feel about

the Sabbath day? I'll share some of my personal reflections with you. When I was young, I wondered just what activities were appropriate for the Sabbath. I read lists of dos and don'ts, all compiled by others. But now I have a much better understanding, which I gained from two Old Testament scriptures. One is from the book of Exodus:

"The Lord spake unto Moses, saying, . . . my sabbaths ye shall keep: for it is a sign between me and you throughout your generations; that ye may know that I am the Lord that doth sanctify you" (Exodus 31:12–13).

A similar message in the book of Ezekiel says:

"I gave them my sabbaths, to be a sign between me and them, that they might know that I am the Lord that sanctify them. . . . I am the Lord your God; . . . hallow my Sabbaths; and they shall be a sign between me and you, that ye may know that I am the Lord your God" (Ezekiel 20:12, 19–20).

Pondering these scriptures has helped me to understand. My behavior on the Sabbath constitutes my sign to the Lord of my regard for Him and for my covenants with Him. If, on the one hand, my interests on the Sabbath day turn to activities such as pro football games or worldly movies, the sign from me to Him would clearly be that my devotions do not favor Him. If, on the other hand, my Sabbath interests focus on the Lord and His teachings, on the family, and on folks who are sick or poor or needy, the sign would likewise be evident to God. I have concluded that our activities on the Sabbath will be appropriate when we honestly consider them to be our personal sign of commitment to the Lord.

Next, Richard, prepare to do work of real worth for your fellow men. The critical difference between your just *hoping* for good things for mankind and your *being able* to do good things for mankind is education.

I'll share another personal reflection. Many years ago when I was a young intern, we had a wonderful neighbor lady named Netta Davis. She had a serious heart condition—a diseased mitral valve destroyed in her youth by the ravages of rheumatic fever. Her husband, Don, was a fellow physician. Because he and I were usually at the hospital, Netta and my sweetheart, Dantzel, became very close friends. Sadly, as the years went by, Netta's strength ebbed, her congestive heart failure worsened, and her little body finally died because of this malfunctioning valve.

This was long before the advent of surgical repairs within the heart. Such was hardly dreamed of in those days. But Netta's passing changed my life. I determined that her death was not to have been in vain.

Then I joined forces with a small team of researchers at a well-known university. Together we embarked on a project to develop an artificial heart-lung machine, as I mentioned earlier. The ultimate purpose of this effort was to allow repairs to be made within the empty heart while the circulation of the patient's blood was temporarily maintained by the apparatus we were developing.

To make connectors for tubing, I learned quite a bit about glassblowing. And I learned how to operate lathes, drill presses, and other machines required to make pumps, valves, and cylinders. With my associates, I also had to learn the physiological requirements for oxygenation of the blood and the requirements for blood flow to, and oxygen consumption of, the tissues. We had to learn how to control coagulation of the blood and then reverse the anticoagulation so normal clotting could again be restored. And we learned the hard way that bacterial contamination could destroy an otherwise successful experiment. Incidentally, the project for my Ph.D. thesis comprised the conquering of that problem.

Long years elapsed before we were able to graduate from the laboratory to practical application in the operating room of a hospital. But finally it happened in 1951. The human heart could be opened. In the years that followed, thanks also to research in laboratories and clinics at many other universities, defective valves and other components could be repaired. The pioneering road was long and rugged. More than eight years elapsed from the time I received my doctor of medicine degree before I performed the first successful open-heart operation here in Utah in 1955.

Netta Davis did not die in vain. Her desperate need motivated me as nothing else could. I thought of her the day I operated upon the heart of President Spencer W. Kimball. In a real sense, it was partially because of Netta that I was able to perform the operation that President Kimball needed.

So, Richard, maintain your motivation and perseverance to do work of worth. It will be a measure of your individual righteousness. No matter what your career may be, the long hours of sacrifice and effort required to achieve excellence are really worth it.

Meanwhile, in your quest for personal righteousness, go periodically to the mountain of the Lord's house—His holy temple. There, learn of Him. Covenant with Him. There and wherever you are, pray to our Heavenly Father in the name of His Son. Merge your faith with your scholarship to give a spiritual depth of focus to all of your righteous desires. Richard, if you will do these things, you will develop an "eye single to the glory of God" (D&C 4:5). Then you will really have 20/20 vision!

As we all contemplate resolutions for our lives, let us reflect on a special behavioral blueprint given by revelation to the Prophet Joseph Smith. These verses from the 88th section of the Doctrine and Covenants are worthy resolutions equally applicable in our day. The Lord said:

"Cease from all your light speeches, . . . from all your lustful desires, from all your pride and light-mindedness, and from all your wicked doings. . . .

"See that ye love one another; cease to be covetous; learn to impart one to another as the gospel requires.

"Cease to be idle; cease to be unclean; cease to find fault one with another; cease to sleep longer than is needful; retire to thy bed early, that ye may not be weary; arise early, that your bodies and your minds may be invigorated.

"And above all things, clothe yourselves with the bond of charity, as with a mantle, which is the bond of perfectness and peace.

"Pray always, that ye may not faint, until I come. Behold, and lo, I will come . . . and receive you unto myself" (D&C 88:121, 123–26).

Learn from your personal reflections. Let them help you understand who you are, from where you have come, and what God expects you to be. Then let your resolutions strengthen your future. Feast on the words of Christ. Apply His teachings in your lives. Then you will achieve your greatest potential for good.

NOTE

From a Brigham Young University fireside address, January 1990.

17

Now Is the Time
to Prepare

On February 13, 2005, my sweetheart—my beloved wife of fifty-nine years—passed away. While I was at home on a rare Saturday with no assignment, we had worked together. She had washed our clothing. I had helped to carry it, fold it, and put it in place. Then while we were sitting on the sofa, holding hands, enjoying a program on television, my precious Dantzel slipped peacefully into eternity.

Her passing came suddenly and unexpectedly. Just four days earlier, our doctor's report at a routine checkup indicated that her laboratory tests were good. After my efforts to revive her proved fruitless, feelings of shock and sorrow overwhelmed me. My closest friend, angel mother of our ten children, grandmother of our fifty-six grandchildren, had been taken from us.

Dantzel was not only a loved and loving companion but also a teacher. By her noble example she taught faith, virtue, obedience, and mercy. She taught me how to listen and to love. Because of her, I know all the blessings that can come to a husband, father, and grandfather.

From her sudden departure we can learn a very important lesson: Now is the time to prepare to meet God. Tomorrow may be too late. Prophets through the ages have so declared: "This life is the time for men to prepare to meet God. . . . Do not procrastinate the day of your repentance" (Alma 34:32–33; see also Alma 13:27).

The Need to Prepare Now

Yet many do procrastinate.[1] A prophet has warned us: "Ye cannot say . . . that I *will* repent, that I *will* return to my God. Nay, ye cannot say this; for that same spirit which doth possess your bodies at the time that ye go out of this life, that same spirit will . . . possess your body in that eternal world" (Alma 34:34; emphasis added). Another prophet adds, "He that is filthy shall be filthy still; and he that is righteous shall be righteous still" (Mormon 9:14; see also 2 Nephi 9:15–16; D&C 88:27–32, 34–35; 130:2).

Great is the knowledge that "whatever principle of intelligence we attain . . . in this life, it will rise with us in the resurrection" (D&C 130:18). From the Prophet Joseph Smith we also learn that "God has . . . a time . . . appointed . . . when He will bring all His subjects, who have obeyed His voice and kept His commandments, into His celestial rest. This rest[2] is of such perfection and glory, that man has need of a preparation before he can, according to the laws of that kingdom, enter it and enjoy its blessings. . . . God has given certain laws to the human family, which, if observed, are sufficient to prepare them to inherit this rest."[3] Sister Nelson was so prepared!

That glorious goal seems mighty distant if one is discouraged by worldly trouble and gloom. I remember when a friend having a difficult day exclaimed, "Oh, why was I ever born?" God's plan answers his question. We came into this life to acquire a physical body. We may fall in love and be married. We may have children and experience the trials of mortal life.[4] The Church was restored—the earth was created—so that families could be sealed in holy temples. Otherwise, the whole earth would be "utterly wasted" (D&C 2:1–3; 138:48; Joseph Smith—History 1:39).

We came to be tried, to be tested, and to choose (2 Nephi 9:27; D&C 98:12; Abraham 3:24–26). Our decisions determine our destiny. We are "free to choose liberty and eternal life, through the great Mediator . . . , or to choose captivity and death" (2 Nephi 2:27). Those who choose the Lord's way will likely endure persecution (2 Timothy 3:12). But their reward is certain. Those who prove faithful "shall inherit the kingdom of God, . . . and their joy shall be full forever" (2 Nephi 9:18). Sister Nelson has earned that reward. What comfort that brings to our family and me!

Trials and tests apply to rich and poor alike. Years ago I was asked to perform an operation upon a very wealthy man. A surgical biopsy confirmed that he had an advanced cancer that had spread throughout his body. As I reported this news, his immediate response was to rely upon his wealth. He would go anywhere or do anything to treat his condition. He thought he could buy his way back to health. But he soon passed away. Someone asked, "How much wealth did he leave?" The answer, of course, was, "All of it!"

His priorities were set upon things of the world. His ladder of success had been leaning against the wrong wall. I think of him when I read this scripture: "Behold, your days of probation are past; ye have procrastinated the day of your salvation until it is . . . too late" (Helaman 13:38).

In radiant contrast, Sister Nelson prepared throughout her life for the time when she would return to God. She lived each day as though it were her last. She cherished every hour, knowing that time on earth is precious.

Some people live as if there were no day of reckoning. Others waste today's time with a disabling fear of tomorrow or a paralyzing preoccupation over mistakes of yesterday. Each of us might well heed the words of a poet, as posted on a sundial:

> *The shadow by my finger cast*
> *Divides the future from the past:*
> *Before it, sleeps the unborn hour,*
> *In darkness, and beyond thy power:*
> *Behind its unreturning line,*
> *The vanished hour, no longer thine:*
> *One hour alone is in thy hands,—*
> *The NOW on which the shadow stands.*[5]

How Do We Prepare?

Now is the time, but *how* do we prepare? Begin with repentance! Scripture declares, "If ye have sought to do wickedly in the days of your probation, then ye are found unclean before the judgment-seat of God; . . . no unclean thing can dwell with God" (1 Nephi 10:21). He gave this simple rule: "Except ye abide my law ye cannot attain to this glory" (D&C 132:21; see also D&C 88:36–39).

Now is the time to show reverent respect for one's physical

body. It serves as the tabernacle for one's spirit throughout all eternity. Physical appetites are to be controlled by the will of one's spirit. We are to "deny [our]selves of all ungodliness" (Moroni 10:32; see also 2 Nephi 2:21; Mormon 9:28). We are to "forsake all evil and cleave unto all good, [and] live by every word which proceedeth forth out of the mouth of God" (D&C 98:11).

Because of frequent and frightening calamities in the world, some people doubt the existence of God. But, in fact, He is trying to help us. He revealed these words: "How oft have I called upon you by the mouth of my servants, and by the ministering of angels, and by mine own voice, and by the voice of thunderings, and . . . tempests, . . . earthquakes, . . . great hailstorms, . . . famines and pestilences of every kind, . . . and would have saved you with an everlasting salvation, but ye would not!" (D&C 43:25).

His hope for us is eternal life. We qualify for it by obedience to covenants and ordinances of the temple—for ourselves, our families, and our ancestors. We cannot be made perfect without them (D&C 128:15, 18). We cannot *wish* our way into the presence of God. We are to obey the laws upon which those blessings are predicated (D&C 130:20–21).

God's plan is fair. Even those "who have died without a knowledge of this gospel, who would have received it if they had been permitted to tarry, shall be heirs of the celestial kingdom of God" (D&C 137:7). His plan is also merciful. He "will judge all men according to their works, according to the desire of their hearts" (D&C 137:9).

Now is the time to enroll our names among the people of God. This we do by paying tithing. He tithes His people to bless them (Malachi 3:10; 3 Nephi 24:10).[6] Sister Nelson taught that lesson to our family over and over again.[7]

Now is the time to align our goals with God's goals. His work and His glory—"to bring to pass the immortality and eternal life of man" (Moses 1:39; see also Moses 6:59; JST, Genesis 6:62)—can become ours. Of temple marriage the Savior declared, "If a man marry a wife by my word, which is my law, and by the new and everlasting covenant, . . . [they] shall inherit thrones, kingdoms, principalities, and powers, dominions, . . . exaltation and glory in all things" (D&C 132:19; see also D&C 75:5; 101:65). We are to emulate the example of the Lord, to love as He did, to pray as He did, and to endure to the end as He did (2 Nephi 33:4; 3 Nephi 15:9; 27:21–22; D&C 14:7).

The Importance of Death in God's Eternal Plan

Death is a necessary component of our eternal existence. No one knows when it will come, but it is essential to God's great plan of happiness (Alma 42:8–9). Thanks to the Atonement of the Lord, eventual resurrection is a reality, and eternal life is a possibility for all humankind (1 Corinthians 15:50–54; 1 John 5:11, 20; Alma 12:25; Mormon 9:13; D&C 46:14; 76:40–42, 50–59; 133:62). That possibility becomes a reality as we obey God's law. He said, "Except ye shall keep my commandments, . . . ye shall in no case enter into the kingdom of heaven" (3 Nephi 12:20). One day we will be judged by the Lord (1 Nephi 10:20; 2 Nephi 9:41–46; Alma 12:27) and go to our own mansion prepared in our Father's heavenly house (John 14:2; D&C 98:18). Celestial glory awaits those who have been faithful to God's gentle commands (D&C 78:7; 131:1–3).

We live to die and we die to live—in another realm. If we

are well prepared, death brings no terror. From an eternal perspective, death is premature only for those who are not prepared to meet God.

Now is the time to prepare. Then, when death comes, we can move toward the celestial glory that Heavenly Father has prepared for His faithful children. Meanwhile, for sorrowing loved ones left behind—such as our family and me—the sting of death is soothed by a steadfast faith in Christ, a perfect brightness of hope, a love of God and of all men, and a deep desire to serve them (2 Nephi 31:20; Mosiah 16:7–8; Moroni 7:38–48).

That faith, that hope, that love will qualify us to come into God's holy presence and, with our eternal companions and families, dwell with Him forever.

NOTES

From a talk given at general conference, April 2005.

1. Scripture admonishes each of us to "harden not [our] hearts any longer; for behold, now is the time and the day of your salvation; . . . therefore, if ye will repent . . . , immediately shall the great plan of redemption be brought about unto you" (Alma 34:31).
2. In the New Testament, the term *rest* has been translated from the Greek feminine noun *katapausis,* which means "the heavenly blessedness in which God dwells." Thus, *rest* connotes an element of glory.
3. *Teachings of the Prophet Joseph Smith,* sel. Joseph Fielding Smith (Salt Lake City: Deseret Book, 1976), 54.
4. Please forgive me for mentioning children and the trials of life in the same breath. I sense that they are both part of our growing process.
5. Henry Van Dyke, "The Sun-Dial at Wells College," in *The Poems of Henry Van Dyke* (New York: Charles Scribner's Sons, 1911), 345. Sundial and poem displayed at Wells College in Aurora, New York.
6. Tithing also prepares people against a future day of vengeance and burning (D&C 85:3).
7. Spencer J. Condie, *Russell M. Nelson: Father, Surgeon, Apostle* (Salt Lake City: Deseret Book, 2003), 104.

18

"Neither Trust
in the Arm of Flesh"

As long as you live, you will learn. It is part of God's plan for us. You will grow intellectually and spiritually. Just as Jesus the Christ "increased in wisdom and stature, and in favour with God and man" (Luke 2:52), so may you.

To increase your wisdom and stature, you will exercise your agency. You will choose your teachers and role models. Choose them wisely. Heed this counsel of Alma: "Trust no one to be your teacher . . . except he be a man of God, walking in his ways and keeping his commandments" (Mosiah 23:14).

People who are entering the job market now do so at a time of economic distress. Job opportunities throughout the world are diminishing and becoming more competitive. You will need to work hard and perform well to hold a job in the difficult days that lie ahead.

The decline of our economy is affecting many. Senior

citizens who have retired from their work are strained because the value of their nest egg has been substantially eroded.

Such economic woes are not new. Verses recorded long ago in the Book of Mormon apply today. From Helaman we read, "The time cometh that . . . your riches . . . become slippery, that ye cannot hold them; and in the days of your poverty ye cannot retain them. . . . Yea, in that day ye shall say: O that we had remembered the Lord our God in the day that he gave us our riches, and then they would not have become slippery that we should lose them; for behold, our riches are gone from us" (Helaman 13:31–33).

Throughout history economic conditions have been cyclic in nature. So you will live to see more ups and downs in the economy, just as surely as you will see the seasons change.

With the cycles of man and nature all about us, we need to remember that truth never changes. God lives. He is our Father. He loves us and wants us to be happy. Because He loves us, He wants us to prepare well now for our eventual return to Him. Can you imagine anything more joyful than that homecoming? It truly will be glorious for those who have qualified for the blessings of eternal life.[1]

To assist us in that quest, we have been given help through the teachings of God's prophets and the scriptures. Here is one example: "Cursed is he that putteth his trust in man, or maketh flesh his arm" (2 Nephi 28:31). To rephrase that in today's terms, if you trust only in your 401(k)s or IRAs, your retirement plans may be disappointing. But your investments in tithing will continue to pay rich dividends—here and hereafter. Indeed, the nest egg of tithing will never be eroded.

We learn more about the limitations of the arm of flesh from the Doctrine and Covenants. In its preface we read that "the weak things of the world shall come forth and break down the mighty and strong ones, that man should not counsel his fellow man, neither trust in the arm of flesh" (D&C 1:19). Or to rephrase that warning, even though you may be learned in the ways of the world, don't forget the power of God.

My medical school classmates and I learned that lesson in an unforgettable way more than thirty years ago. We will never forget it. Our experience took place in the little town of Manzanillo, on Mexico's western coast. The year was 1978. We were attending a meeting with our medical school graduating class and their wives.

One evening after the scientific sessions had been completed, one of the doctors suddenly became seriously ill. Without warning, he began to lose massive amounts of blood from his stomach. Totally stunned, we surrounded him, watching life's precious blood flow from him. There we were, medical specialists skilled in various disciplines, including surgeons, anesthesiologists, and internists—each with wisdom gained through more than thirty years of experience. What could we do? The nearest hospital was in Guadalajara, more than one hundred mountainous miles away. It was night. No planes could fly. Blood transfusions were out of the question because of lack of equipment. All of our combined knowledge could not be mobilized to stop his hemorrhage. We were totally without the facilities or equipment needed to save the life of our beloved friend.

Our stricken colleague, a faithful Latter-day Saint, was well aware of his plight. Ashen and pale, he whispered a request for the administration of a priesthood blessing. Several of us held the Melchizedek Priesthood. We responded to his request immediately. I was asked to seal the anointing. The Spirit dictated that he be blessed to the end that the bleeding would stop and that he would continue to live and return to his home. That blessing was administered in the name of the Lord.

The next morning, his condition had improved. Miraculously, the bleeding had stopped. His blood pressure had returned to normal. In a couple of days he was able to return to his home. Unitedly, we thanked the Lord for this most remarkable blessing.

The lesson we learned was simple: "Trust in the Lord with all thine heart; and lean not unto thine own understanding" (Proverbs 3:5). We experienced it firsthand. This doctrine, taught repeatedly in the scriptures (Proverbs 11:28; Jeremiah 17:5; Romans 8:1; 2 Nephi 4:34–35; 2 Nephi 28:31; D&C 1:19–23), had now become our sure knowledge.

Please do not misunderstand me. Of course we need to prepare for worthy work to do. Yes, we do need to do our work well, whatever we choose to do in life. We need to be able to render significant service. And before we can achieve that competence, we need an education. With us, education is a religious responsibility. "The glory of God [really] is intelligence" (D&C 93:36).

But the learning of man has its limitations. And sometimes, as in our circumstance in rural Mexico, the combined learning of many experts cannot be applied when we need it most. We have to place our trust in the Lord.

That experience in Mexico taught us another important lesson. It pertains to our ultimate priorities and highest destinies as mortal beings. We learned that a doctor's ultimate destination is not in the hospital. For a lawyer, it is not in the courtroom. For a jet pilot, it is not in the cockpit of a Boeing 747. Each person's chosen occupation is only a *means* to an end; it is not an end in itself.

The end for which each of you should strive is to be the

person you can become—the person God wants you to be. The day will come when your professional career will end, as it has already for me. The career that you will have labored so hard to achieve—the work that will have supported you and your family—will one day be behind you.

Then you will have learned this great lesson: Much more important than what you have done for a living is what kind of a person you have become. On your final graduation day—when you leave this frail existence—what you have become will matter most. Attributes such as "faith, virtue, knowledge, temperance, patience, brotherly kindness, godliness, charity, humility, [and] diligence" (D&C 4:6) will all be weighed in the Lord's balance.

Keep learning and preparing for your ultimate graduation day (Alma 34:33). From time to time ask yourself these questions: "Am I ready to meet my Maker?" "Am I worthy of all the blessings He has in store for His faithful children?" "Have I received my endowment and sealing ordinances of the temple?" "Have I remained faithful to my covenants?" "Have I qualified for the greatest of all God's blessings—the blessing of eternal life?" (D&C 14:7).

Long ago Moses and the children of Israel sang this song together: "The Lord is my strength . . . he is . . . my salvation: he is my God" (Exodus 15:2; see also JST, Exodus 15:2). I hope that we can all sing that song with equal conviction.

Those who cherish their faith in God—those who trust in Him—have been given this scriptural promise:

"Let no man glory in man, but rather let him glory in God. . . . These shall dwell in the presence of God and his Christ forever and ever" (D&C 76:61–62).

That this may be the ultimate destiny for each of us is my humble prayer.

NOTES

From a Brigham Young University commencement address, April 2009.

1. It will also be dear to our Heavenly Parents. The Psalmist wrote, "Precious in the sight of the Lord is the death of his saints" (Psalm 116:15).

Index